LIKE FALLEN SNOW

LIKE FALLEN SNOW

Memoir with Poetry

RUTH ROSENTHAL

PM Books

Ruth Rosenthal won The American Pen Women Award, Best Short Story of the Year for "Locked Inside" which she read at the San Francisco Main Library.

Copyright © 2010 by Ruth Rosenthal

ISBN: 978-0-9827343-3-9

All rights reserved. No part of this book may be used or reproduced in any manner whatsoever without written permission, except in the case of quotes for personal use and brief quotations embodied in critical articles or reviews.

PM Books
an imprint of Poetic Matrix Press
www.poeticmatrixpress.com

Acknowdledgments

I am grateful for the people and experiences whose stories I share here. They have offered me inspiration and insight. I hope you may find it so for yourself.

I appreciate the editing of Ginny Coffman, Jan Bryon, and Jen Ewing, who brought this book to a fine dimension of completeness.

Credit for planting the seed of its production goes to Karen Freeman, who urged me to do what I had been dreaming of.

Cover photo of Yosemite by Jan Bryon.

Contents

Acknowdledgments
Hail To You, My Dear Brother, Lou   3
Love is Why We Are: Make the Most of It   5
A Day Job   13
A Day Job   14
The Words In My Head   16
Slivovitz   17
A Gift   20
After Breakfast: He Speaks   21
Acceptance   24
Locked Inside   25
Outside My Window   28
The Temple Where Little Girls Worshipped   29
When Bobby and Bobbie Made Music Together   30
From the Bijou to Old Uncle Gaylord's   31
A Poet Needs Words   36
Office Visit   37
Cool It   40
I Think His Name Was Hans   41
Lady of the Birds   43
Where's Your Peacock?   44
How Ruth Felt   47
Savoring   48
Knowing   52
Trusting   53
Cadence   56
Pianta   57
A Song for My Daughter   60
The Quiet One   62
One Morning   66
St. Michael's Waiting Room   69
The Kiss   72
The Vase   73
Extraordinary Dreaming   75

Extraordinary Dreaming	76
Dr. Katzoff On Safety of Kissing	81
Smidgen John	83
I Know	86
Joe's Story	87
Ruth, Then and Now	90
The Waiting Room	92
Waiting for a Friend to Pick Up her Prescription	95
With Hands Out	97
In Court School	101
In the Midst of Plenty	102
One More Story	104
Freedom	106
In the Garden of Life	108
Some of the Sounds of the Universe	109
My Brain	111
I Don't Know Why	112
Equinox	118
The Thrift Shop	119
The Marvelousness	122
What We Liked Best	123
Thursday is Thanksgiving A Mother's Voice	125
Revealment	126
Passion Flower	129
L.A. Dreams	130
Music	132
Jazzman	133
Rumi and I	134
When I Realize That I had become a Grown-up	135
Il Piccolo	137
A Gift from Alice	138
I'd Rather Laugh	141
Dumpster Shoes	143
Reflection	146
Eternity	147

Biography

DEDICATED TO MY BROTHER,

LOU, OF SHINING CHARACTER.

Hail To You, My Dear Brother, Lou

In years past, I wrote proudly,
"My brother was always a hero to me."
And now I see more of you
than I could even see back then.
You are a hero as much
in life's peaceful trauma
as ever you were in war.
You are unflinching, often
uncomprehended,
ultimately giving.
Where need is there,
you give your full heart's worth
of loving care.
I marvel at your incredible
endurance.
Your steadfast focus reflects
the inner strength of you.
Hail to you, my dear brother, Lou.

Love is Why We Are: Make the Most of It

My brother has been interviewed many times. His story is in several books and videos. This story is to share some of the "other parts" which have not been in print, or other media.

I can't imagine what it must be like to be a prisoner. My brother Lou could tell you. He was a prisoner of war for over thirteen months during World War II in Germany. He enlisted in the United States Air Force the day after Pearl Harbor was bombed on December 7, 1941. He didn't have to report for duty until December 26, when he left for Fort Dix, the day before my eleventh birthday.

Our parents, I say "our parents" with a chuckle and a smile, because Lou used to say, "My mother" or "My father," even, "My parents" until I teased him relentlessly, saying, "Our father," or "Our mother" ... you get the picture. He's improving, and our little "family joke" gets us laughing at ourselves.

Our parents came to America from Kiev, Russia in their teens, around 1906. Mom was about sixteen and Pop a couple of years older. There were no birth records back then for them. They first met in New York City where they lived the difficult lives that immigrants did. No English, hardly any money, no government benefits, and to escape to the United States, they suffered—only able to afford the lowest deck aboard ships sailing to America, called steerage, enduring all the difficulties and discomforts that came with it.

Escape—Our mother shared too few words with me about her life. About forty years after her harrowing trip, she simply and unemotionally said one day, "I was escaping from the pogrom."

"What's a pogrom?" I asked.

She said, "The czar came into the village on his horse, killing people."

One day mom told me that the butcher's son helped her learn to read, and write a little, too. The only thing I ever saw her write was her name: Jennie Loevsky. It was legible and neat. The only thing I ever saw her read was the New York Daily Newspaper.

Pop was quite a handsome man—from old pictures I've seen—and have—of them, from when he was "courting" mom, as they called it then. In one sepia photo he was playing the mandolin to her in a park.

He was an extremely hard worker, first for employers, then for himself. One family joke was that when he worked twelve hours, he was working only half a day. Twelve hours, to him, was a short workday. He used to rise at three AM, walk to his shop, and work till ten or eleven PM each day.

Perhaps my addiction to travel came from two people I loved and love: Pop and Lou. The only times Pop took a day off were to go to a wedding or a funeral. After mom died, Pop said he would travel. It was too late. He followed her a year later.

When Lou went into training in the air force he began sending me special gifts from the various places he visited from wherever he was stationed. One gift was a loose jacket with applique scenes on it. One of the colorful scenes, on the back of the jacket, was of a woman doing a Mexican hat dance. I wanted to wear it to school every day, I liked it so well, and the fact that Lou expressed his caring with things I always loved.

Another gift, a flat pair of leather, pointed shoes, from Morocco, was something I only wore in the house so they wouldn't wear out. I wore them so much that, even so, they had to wear out. When I took them to a shoemaker for new soles I was terribly disappointed when he said it couldn't be done.

When I got to Morocco many years later I bought myself a pair. Unlike the ones Lou had sent, they weren't soft and pliable. They were pretty, but hard and uncomfortable. I kept them anyway. Now they decorate an area on a wall, reminding me of Lou's gift.

There was no deep thought or hesitancy on my part about writing letters to Lou when he enlisted. Writing to him everyday after school was my joy and my job.

The letters came and went for the next four years—Lou's to us, mine for Mom, Pop and me, to Lou.

During the fourth year I was required to write on the form allowed to be sent to prisoners of war. It was called V-Mail. Most of my letters were as newsy as I could be and encouraging. But there were a few when I expressed my anger at my brother having to be imprisoned. Those parts, of course, were blacked out by a censor, a German woman whose job it was. She was about Lou's age, twenty-three, or maybe a few years younger.

Many years later, almost half a century, Lou met the censor herself, who was in the States from Germany. She was at his banquet table at a POW reunion. Lou had the photo I'd mailed to him—my school picture from my freshman year in high school. He had kept the picture on the wall above his bunk in Stalag Luft III.

I guess I'd always known that Lou loved me, even though I was beyond what might be called "shy." I was quite withdrawn, and cried a lot as a child. But, if I ever had any doubt about his love, I was well assured when Lou described my photo that had become a "pin-up." He called me beautiful. I am very visual, and when the cameraman had posed me and told me to look away from the camera I couldn't comply. One eye did as I was directed. The other eye looked straight ahead at the camera. I wouldn't think Lou could have thought "beautiful" looking up from his POW hard bunk, made of a thin layer of wood, with some straw, like some strange sandwich, over another layer of wood. But he said it those many years later.

The blankets that were issued to POW's were thin, holey World War I blankets that could literally be seen through, not only the holes, but the rest of it, too. When the Red Cross was expected to check out how things were going for the soldiers, the jailers took away those blankets and issued nice new ones. Once the Red Cross was gone, the new were promptly replaced with the old.

Lou, not a person to be daunted, was ready for the next time. He cut a length about a foot wide from the new blanket and hid it. One of his military peer officers warned him that he could be court marshaled for that. Reluctantly, but sensibly, Lou agreed. But he still had his cut piece of new blanket.

The March—The winter of 1943 was so bitter cold that the piece of chocolate Lou had stashed for a time when he might need it most, was frozen solid. They marched from Stalag Luft III to Mooseburg, fatigued and malnourished at the start from meals of bread made with 50% sawdust and from watered down soups. When the Red Cross tried to help out and sent packages of nutritious food, Lou's captors told them that because of America's bombings, no such packages ever arrived. On Liberation Day, by General Patton, and his soldiers, a warehouse full of Red Cross confiscated packages were found.

If a soldier, in good health at the start, in the low to mid twenties of age, weighing 180 pounds, lost a pound a day, in three months time, dead or alive, his weight would be only 90 pounds. This happened. This is no mere math talk.

Lou is a survivor. His "stolen" piece of blanket went with him on that awful winter's march. He had a scarf made from it, over his head, around his neck, across his chest. And his own fashioned mittens.

They were given a large loaf of the half sawdust bread, for twenty men and devised a fair way to share it amongst themselves. Each time a different man sliced the loaf as thinly as he could. Like the World War I blankets, you could see through the bread, too. The man who sliced the bread that day got the last slice.

Because of their deathly diet, healthy young men were paying a high price—not condoned or acceptable by the Geneva Convention.

In the cattle cars they were packed into, on their way to prison camps, soldiers had no space in which to squat so they could use the only metal can provided for all of them. In prison camp, where he could defecate only once a week, Lou described it as like a brick with rough edges and bleeding. One time when he left the latrine, which was a walk from their barracks, he was halfway between latrine and barracks, when the air raid siren screeched. No one was outside. He had to quickly decide whether to run back to the latrine or to the barracks. He ran for the barracks. When Lou got there, before bombs began falling, the door was locked. He called out to be let in. The U. S. Lt. Colonel inside yelled back, "Don't come in." Lou kicked the door down, stepped over his service superior and kept walking. The Lt. Colonel, furious, shouted, "I'll have you court marshaled for this." Lou's answer: silence.

As a kid I loved it when Lou, almost eleven years older, invited me to join him. I didn't care where or for what. I still feel the same way.

One typical very hot, muggy summer day in New Jersey, in the town of Lyndhurst, where we lived, Lou asked if I'd like to go to the Lyndhurst Community Pool with him. Of course! He taught me how to roll my bathing suit into a towel and we were off. At the last minute Lou asked me if I'd like to go swimming in the Passaic River, nearby, instead. Better yet, I thought.

The water felt so soothing in the heat as I eagerly followed Lou into the river. The soft, smooth mud bottom of the river felt great to my bare feet. All of a sudden he turned and told me to get out of the water. I asked, "Why?" as I did. Then I saw why. He was well-covered by tar from boats that used the river, and up to as far as I'd gotten in, so was I. I didn't mind. This was an adventure with my brother, better than the public pool could ever be.

Back in U.S. training camps, Lou's service peers would complain a lot. When Lou had enlisted, the recruiter lowered a huge map of the United States and asked him where he'd like to go to begin his training. Since he liked warm weather and swimming, he chose Biloxi, Mississippi. His service peers were all upset: the water didn't taste good. Mosquitoes were biting. Nothing was any good. Lou, my "make the best of it" brother, would pack some underwear, shaving items, five dollars of his twenty-one dollar monthly government allotment, all into his small GI shaving kit, and enjoy his leave.

Not always was there a pass for a leave so Lou left anyway—Absent Without Official Leave (AWOL). He did this in a clever way that didn't draw attention, right in front of those chatting officers who didn't pay enough attention to Lou's attitude. His way of functioning more than helped him when he was taken prisoner.

The prisoners received seeds to plant. They were provided by an organization on the order of the Red Cross through the International YMCA, whose headquarters were in Switzerland. Commanding Officer Spivey saw to it that the men were provided with some musical instruments and they were allotted a meager amount of bats and balls to keep them active, healthy and amused.

Their guards had no used for the seeds. Some of the prisoners were gathering "night soil" for fertilizer. But they had a scarce supply of water. Lou noticed the latrine had an overhead container of water that he wanted to use for the seeds. How to get it working for his goal? He saw some hosing, ignored by everyone, that he decided to use, but he needed something else to make it work. He saw that "something else" in a heavy log that had been left out by the German military. Lou walked to the log with a wheel barrow that was sitting around, managed to get the heavy log onto the wheelbarrow and walked, head down but assertive, like that was his job as one of their camp assistants. Two guards were busy talking to each other. As Lou did, when he went AWOL in the States, he walked right between them and did what he wanted.

When he got the wood to his barracks he patiently made it into the small pieces he needed in order to form a conduit for the water to flow from the overhead toilet tank into the place where he'd planted the seeds. Those seeds were soon flourishing.

Lou is his own man, regardless of circumstances. His fellow captives, watching him and judging, soon began saying, "Lou's gone around the bend again."

To keep from the boredom of captivity and the uncertainty of life as a maltreated POW, he went outside one day and placed some little bits of sweetening on the tips of all his fingers. Sitting quietly, patiently, he soon—one by one—was feeding ten hungry bees. Freer than he, they were, but he had kept his mind focused, as always, living his hellish reality the best way he could. "Lou's gone around the bend again."

When their B-24 was shot down over Berlin the sixteen year old German soldier who had shot it, disobeyed orders by leaving his post, and took a "shot" with his camera of the downed plane's serial number for proof of his accomplishment. Over half a century later Lou and—Harry was his name—met. It was at another of the POW's reunions in the States. Harry had family in America and made it his business to contact Lou when he came to see his family.

With many years between, Lou had come to the point of forgiveness where all good things can begin, and agreed to the meeting. As Lou, in his delightful sense of the ridiculous, put it, "If I can walk down the aisle" (at his daughter's wedding) "with my ex-wife, I can meet the guy who shot my plane down."

And so they met, with Lou's second wife Molly and Harry's wife. It must have felt like a cleansing of bitter memories put to rest. It seems like Harry had peace to make with both Lou and himself. They all looked forward to another meeting in another year. Before that time, Harry passed on, freed of a lifetime's weight of conscience.

When Lou was about seventy-seven, he called me up and said that he might be awarded the Distinguished Flying Cross. He said, "If it happens, I hope it's while I'm still alive."

When he was twenty-three and their plane was shot, they had to bail out. Len Smith, the bombardier, was trapped in the nose turret. He was in shock and began removing his oxygen mask and gloves (at -35 degrees or below, at 23,000 feet.) Lou kept trying to put Len's mask and gloves back on repeatedly, while trying to spring the nose turret door open. It couldn't open. Finally, Lou dragged Len out to safety through the bomb bay. He survived and they met once again in POW camp.

Lou was never honored in any way for his heroism. His service peers decided that that wasn't right and contacted the government. The government gave two reasons why no Distinguished Flying Cross should be given: it wasn't timely because the rescue took place over half a century before. The other reason had to do with a geographical disparity, as they saw it. Geographically Lou was where he was sent to be. Come on!

So, thanks to Molly's friend, a politician, and with the "persistence of a Lou," his service buddies got Lou justice. Lou was given the choice of a parade with much more 'pomp and circumstance' in his hometown in NJ, or a tribute outside of Savannah, Georgia, at the Mighty 8th Air Force Museum. Lou chose the latter, where more of his air force peers, families and friends could attend.

Of course our small family was proudly there. The local newspaper and TV station interviewed Lou, as did his hometown paper. I wrote an article that was in the San Jose Mercury News called, "My Brother Was Always a Hero To Me."

There are still Air Force and POW reunions. But, as Lou sadly puts it, "Many of them have folded their wings."

Some former POWs have rights and benefits that they're unaware of for both themselves and their spouses. Lou is their self-made, self-elected ombudsman, helping to push aside resistances and red tape, supporting in every way, what he sees that isn't always obvious to others.

Lou has taken on, as his joy and his job, the nurturing of those men still left.

A Day Job

There are voices
angry voices
spilling their dissents.
And a listener
simply listening
to their sad events
makes a difference
makes a difference
in their recompense.

A Day Job

I used to work in offices doing secretarial work. It helped pay the bills. But I always felt, "What am I doing here?"

Office work suddenly became more interesting to me when I became a claims examiner, paying medical claims. The largest account I was given was the San Francisco Yellow Cab Company. It had terrible coverage. Cabbies would call me complaining and angry. I'd give them total compassion and understanding. Their irate voices would calm, and I'd pay their claims the way I had to. One cab driver came in and brought me a small vial of water from Lourdes because my mother had cancer.

There was a very cheerful, nice older man—I thought "older," probably no more than I am now—but I was about thirty then. He had an ombudsman kind of position and tried to keep the cab drivers happy, in spite of their inadequate medical insurance contract.

The office I worked in was on the top floor. I don't remember how many floors were there at the corner of Kearny and Sutter. But I'll never forget every time he came by to see me for a little good-will visit. The elevator opened directly onto the office floor, no lobby, no hallway, or doors to open. I sat at the far end of a huge room, occupied by other claims representatives. My desk was next to a radiator. For some reason it was always hot and couldn't be shut off. So, not to roast, I kept the window open.

The "older" man would always come in from the elevator, greeting me with great gusto, and as he approached, from better than a dozen feet away, he'd rip off his jaunty, beige golf cap, and toss it onto my desk. I'd watch the cap go through the air like a slow motion film, and worry it onto my desk, afraid it would sail right through the open window. It never did.

It was nice to have such a jolly fellow break up a few minutes of a job where I couldn't please our disappointed clients.

Since it was my first such experience, much of the time I'd be on the phone with medical offices, the phone in my left hand, and a medical dictionary in my right. Somehow I'd manage to juggle the heavy Physicians' Desk Reference as well.

It seems that all of the cabbies went to the same doctor, and no matter their symptoms or illnesses, the first visit included a proctoscopy—not paid by insurance. This digital probe of a most private area was the joke of the office before I'd ever heard of Connecticut General Insurance Company. So I felt it was as much my job to soothe my angry callers as it was to deny their payments.

I was newly remarried when interviewed for the position. My prospective employer emphasized two things. She wanted a mature person to handle their accounts, especially the cab company. And she practically had me swear on a bible that I wouldn't get pregnant!

I let her think I was mature by not saying too much, and assured her I wasn't planning to become pregnant. She must have been surprised when another employee who was verging on menopause, and already had twelve kids, became pregnant. So was the employee.

There was a cab driver who had phoned several times disturbed about his insurance coverage. He had a deep, smooth, beautiful voice. But when he told me he was coming into the office I was frankly disturbed. He was not happy at all with a three dollar payment toward a bill in the hundreds.

He arrived. He was unlike his voice. I wouldn't have pictured him so large and imposing looking. After checking up front he came directly to me. He was there for one purpose.

He brought me something he had made himself - pizza!

The Words In My Head

I grew up with them and thought I was the only one—
a lonely place to be.
The words followed me like a hungry dog,
during classes, at home, wherever I would be.
Their distraction blocked out teachers
till I wondered how I could even get the grades I did
I would shun conversations, gossip, and the media
which seemed so negative.
But I could not lose what I was doing to myself mostly in my head
So I judged the ways of others
when my thoughts were no better than what they said
I felt justified about myself
when they proved wrong when I was right.

I can say this in the past tense as though I'm through with that.
But present is where I reach from here to here.
The journey is as close as my breath, yet feels far as the stars.

Sometimes it takes a crisis.
As I return for inner strength, as I come to acceptance
of the worst and best, the words in my head lead me to the Truth.
I Am.

Slivovitz

Pop used to get up at three in the morning. He walked the four blocks from Second Avenue to his shop in Lyndhurst, NJ. That was the typical way he began each day. The large vat of metal needed hours of intense heat before it would be liquid and ready to be poured into molds. In the early years the molds formed little bridges to be set into the dirt of garden plants. They were sprayed with red lacquer and then hand painted golden tips were added. I liked those tiny, round golden tips. When I was a child, I painted some myself. Another ornament, no bigger than your thumb, which I liked to hold in my hand and do things with my mind, was the round birdbath on a pedestal, with a bird sitting on its edge. I knew that bird, smaller than the smallest feather, painted with a quick dab of blue, like I knew the Big Little Books I loved to read.

But I never really knew Pop. I knew his habits. He was home by ten or eleven in the morning for breakfast. My mother had his coffee, hot, strong and ready. His pickled herring. The rye bread. And slivovitz. Slivovitz and my pop were serious.

The time he ate and drank was his first respite in a long and busy day. He would soon be on his way back to the shop. When his several employees left at the sound of a distant five o'clock horn, which was heard throughout the town, Pop stayed on, spraying boards filled with casted ornaments, or trimming their excess metal, called gates. He had a long legged wooden chair. It must have been my brother Lou who printed "POP" on the backrest. That's where he sat when the rest of the work was done and ornaments, or, in later years, lamp bases or bookends were ready for him to pack and ship by the gross to New York City.

Pop stayed on and worked until ten or eleven at night. He came home, aching tired, to finally eat his dinner. He often couldn't, because I saw that sleep, instead, slipped him away at the dinner table. The times this pattern varied, rarely, Pop would joke when he worked about twelve hours, "Only half a day."

That joke was even more rare an event because Pop was too involved with survival to joke.

We somehow communicated with my mother's help. She was eager to share, to understand, to make things feel right.

I had come back to the house on Second Avenue for the first time in many years. For the first time in his life, Pop was making his own coffee, trying to make it the way he liked it. He was learning to do some cooking, somehow. My mother was in the hospital—again.

It was almost ten in the morning. I was a guest now in the house where I had lived for about eight years from the time I was ten. Pop had just prepared a pot of very strong coffee, with chicory. He had already taken the herring from the refrigerator and bread was beside it.

"Do you want?"

"OK."

"Good."

He poured me a mug of hot, black coffee.

"Herring, too?"

I had enjoyed herring once or twice before in my life, if I took a small bite of herring and a large bite of bread.

"All right."

"Eat. You're not eating much," he poured a jigger sized glass of slivovitz and was about to down it in one gulp, as I had seen him do many times at this kitchen table, when I saw a thought occur to him.

"Do you like slivovitz?"

"What is it made of? I never had it."

"It's made from plums."

"I like plums."

"It's 200 proof."

As he began to pour I began to realize to a small degree what I was getting into. In my childhood I'd heard Pop talk of 80 proof and 100 proof with admiration in his voice. Now he had gone on to stronger proof. And I was just beginning.

I took a larger bite of herring and of bread, as he put back the bottle's stopper. We each lifted our glasses, ("L'chayim," to your health) and I did what I'd seen Pop do many times. I swallowed the deep amber drink in one large gulp. I expected the burning sensation. I had once, as a teenager, tried a schnaps that way. But I didn't expect the great concentration of heat, which felt like I was glowing inside.

Pop was pouring his second slivovitz and asking, "You like it?" sounding so hopeful. This was already ten times more conversation than we had ever had in my whole life all together. I warmed to that more than anything and would do nothing to end that moment before it would be over.

"I like it!"

He actually smiled as he took that as an acceptance of another shot.

I served myself more herring and another slice of bread.

The second shot was no milder, of course. But I'd had the first and knew better what to expect. It went down hot and easy.

What I didn't expect was an offer for a third one. The alcohol had found my head. "It's only ten-thirty and I've had two slivovitz already," I thought. "But today is different," I reasoned. And reason won out. We drank our final drink together, ever.

A Gift

*When it comes to art
I'm a dabbler
and to most of the rest
a dilettante,
but friendship is
a sacred place
a gift
to the soul
which nourishes
and values
the treasure of its being
beyond any tangibles
we can create.*

After Breakfast: He Speaks

Those who come to a certain private music camp in the mountains often say, "It's indescribable." I've said it myself. Entrance, for the past half century or so, is by invitation.

Families look forward, through cold winter months, to July, when they can once again pitch their tents and absorb the music of many cultures, performed on several outdoor stages. It's an option to bring your own food. The "old-timers" know better. You may be a gourmet chef, but the camp food is amazing, with its original delights, vegetarian and not.

If you've been there once before, you will recognize a number of people when you return. People are gregarious and friendly.

Around a pond, and higher into the hills, are colorful tents. There are classes, at no cost, from batiking, to drumming, to learning songs of the Balkans and Africa—from dancing to papermaking to yoga. For children of all ages there are acting classes, with their rehearsed play performed for all to enjoy, this time a combination take-off on "Alice in Wonderland" and "Peter Pan." Their instructor proudly announces that the children accomplished all this in only five days. The small band of adult musicians sit on the floor below the open air stage, looking just as proud as the kids they play for.

One can check the boards where classes and performance schedules are posted. The flamenco is as good as it gets, even in Spain.

There is a sweet mixture of professional musicians and those who play just for the sheer love of it.

Walking dirt paths through the vast expanse of towering trees, one can hear mellow sounds of campers sitting in front of their tents, singing songs that have been around for many years, some never written, simply sung with their old guitars or mandolins, their lutes or flutes.

There is one man, who, when I pass him, shows no warmth or any sort of conviviality. He might be somewhere in his sixties or less. He seems aware and intelligent. He can't help noticing me as we sometimes cross paths. But he is unlike all the others. I wonder about him.

One morning when I arrive for breakfast most tables are full. I want to sit as closely as I can to the violinist who is playing some lovely classical music. In order to do that, I see that the only available table has three empty chairs, one tipped to the table, and, on the table, a cup of coffee with cream in it. I sit beside the chair tipped forward, facing the violinist.

The man shows up. I speak to him for the first time, "Did I take your table?"

He shakes his head no.

I decide not to say anything else to him—yet. We eat in silence, as I did with my father. The man's demeanor reminds me of my lonely childhood. I slipped back into my childhood memories.

I was not permitted to play with other children. The laughter of children next door was painful to me because I wanted to be there, laughing and playing, too. I walked in our yard, touching flowers.

The boy across the street would call me to play with him, but I couldn't. He'd yell, "Wuthie, Wuthie, Wuthie, you're a wat." I'd run inside, crying and tell my mother. She told me to tell him, "Sticks and stones can break my bones, but words can never hurt me." I went back to the curb and did as I was told. But his words DID hurt me.

Even with school, I was treated differently. When my mother first took me to register for kindergarten, the school principal offered her to wait another year. I began kindergarten three months before my seventh birthday.

About a decade later, I understood what must have caused their choices. My mother, in a calm soft voice, told me that when she was sixteen she fled Russia by boat, to escape the pogroms, the killings in her village by the czar.

As a child, there was no laughter at home, barely any other kind of stimulation. I used to walk down the sidewalk in front of our porch, to the street sidewalk and wait there. When people walked by I would simply say, "Hi." Some responded, some did not.

The violin still enhancing my senses, my breakfast finished, I am ready to speak to the man at the table. It surprised me, when he first sat down, to see him remove chewing gum from his mouth and place it on the funky little wood table. Why surprised? He doesn't let anyone in to know him.

When I look into his eyes, he looks present, but no more. As I look again, not speaking, I sense his safe—but leery—communication opening, when he lifts his eyebrows and opens his large blue eyes wider. Steadily he continues eating.

The music finished, I ask, "Did you design your ring?"

"No, my friend did."

I look more closely at the ring which is silver and covers one third of his thick finger up to his knuckle.

He sees I am trying to tell what the design is, and says, "It's a mermaid."

I ask, "How long have you been coming here?"

Slowly he raises his two hands, fingers spread apart. Then he does the same with one hand.

His only facial expression shows in his large eyes, now opened wider, for the second time.

I say, "This is my second year. The only thing I don't like is the noise at night. But I learned there are industrial strength earplugs. I used the ones I had, covered by head phones."

"*Make the best of it*, is my brother's motto, and he knows what that means. He was a prisoner of war. He's my inspiration."

The man, in silence, lifts both thumbs up.

I say, "Nice talking with you," and rise to continue my day.

Acceptance

*If you'd asked me forty years ago when I climbed ragged hills
at oceanside, with a crowbar,
if I could imagine what my todays would be
I could not imagine what is now.
My friend had given me a crowbar
so we could make like hunters of the sea
releasing mussels from their stronghold habitat to put them in a stew.
My friend assured me
this was one of the only safe months to consume them
because it had the letter "r" in it.
Were it a month without an "r" I could not be here to tell this tale
because, according to my friend, mussels are poisonous
from May through the month of August.
The passage of my life finds me more reflective the longer it goes.
There is an old expression about something not being a picnic.
In spite of that meaning, I make my life a picnic
most of the time.
But like a picnic, one can anticipate a litany:
strong wind, rain, ants.
They have arrived like unwelcome visitors,
For our soul's growth, I believe we choose certain experiences
before we arrive at this life.
I keep that in mind now that I feel
like I'm at the other end of that crowbar.
I remember there is always more to grow.
Painful it is when what can't be changed
isn't met with gracious acceptance.
I'm living to learn to do it with grace.*

Locked Inside

I drove too fast to the state psychiatric hospital. I wanted to help but wasn't sure what I would do once I got there. After all, I had no training in this field. The volunteer coordinator had briefed me. The people I would visit were known to smash windows, break furniture and attack each other.

My daughter had been a patient there briefly when she was eighteen. Jaki's mental anguish had become too much for either of us to handle. Now I didn't know where Jaki was. It had been months since she called. She wanted me to know she was OK, but wouldn't say where she was.

I pulled into the parking lot. "What am I doing here?" I said to myself. I felt compelled to do this, but didn't know exactly what I would do or say.

The coordinator greeted me warmly. "I'll take you there myself," she said. We walked down long, narrow hallways—just like all the other psychiatric hospitals I had seen. A sweet, acrid smell lingered, the same odor I remembered from visiting Jaki in other hospitals.

"There is one young man here—Tom. Be especially careful of him," the woman said, leading the way to the large room which was almost devoid of furniture. Bars blocked light from coming through the windows.

"How long has he been here?"

"A year next week."

My throat tightened as the heavy door was opened for me.

"That's him. Do be careful. Don't turn your back to him."

I was told that I would be locked into the room. The ominous high ceiling and gray aura reminded me of the movie "Snake Pit."

Several men hung around, not seeming to notice me, except for Tom. I sat on a bench along the wall, remembering the caution, keeping my eyes on the movement of everyone, especially Tom. He looked at the newly replaced windowpanes. I wondered if he were thinking of smashing a chair into them again.

Tom turned slowly and looked at me again. I sat quietly on the hard wooden bench to his right. As he walked toward me I wondered, "Oh, my God. What did I get myself into?"

Tom stood in front of me. I looked up at his long, thin face and said, "Hi."

No answer.

I was a fragile fawn, waiting. Frozen.

Tom sat down beside me. We examined each other with serious eyes.

"My name is Ruth," I ventured.

Tom sat still. He didn't take his eyes from my face. His eyes seemed to ask why I had come, so I answered, "I came here to visit, to see you and anyone else who would like a visit."

His silence couldn't hide his apparent intelligence. I wondered if Tom threw his food around as he did the chairs. He moved closer. I noticed his shabby, baggy, brown pants as he pressed his hot boney left leg against mine.

"Don't move," I thought. "If I don't move, everything will be all right." I listened to the thoughts that came to me, although I didn't know where they came from.

I smiled at Tom. *I hope he doesn't think I'm flirting*, I thought, constantly aware of his strong thin leg against mine. I said whatever came to me, making conversation, not daring to look away or to move.

Tom lifted my right hand. I watched, almost as if I were watching Tom with another person. He smiled. I let him hold my hand. He wasn't holding it like a lover. He was studying it, like an artist who was getting perspective before painting.

"Look," he said, with pleasure in his voice.

I had been so involved with my emotions, I didn't feel Tom guide my hand next to his.

"Look at our rings," he said.

I looked at the silver ring on Tom's hand. It had intricate designs carved in it—the same design of my ring. Tom laughed in delight for a moment, then caught himself and resumed being quiet and sober. Our legs, still touching, seemed to vibrate together and generate a heat that encompassed my entire being.

Tom smiled, "You felt it too, didn't you?" he asked.

"Yes," I answered with surprise.

"That's because you understood me. Thank you for that."

When it was time to leave, I stood up and said, "I'll come back. I promise." Someone on the other side of the door unlocked it for me. I drove home in the slow lane. I was in no hurry, digesting what had just occurred.

A few days later my contact at the hospital phoned, "How did you do it?" she asked.

"Do what?"

"I can't believe it's the same Tom. Ruth, when he first came here all he did was suck on baby bottles. Then he progressed to violent behavior. But he never, ever said a word until your visit. Now he talks to everyone."

"Thank you for telling me."

I knew what had helped Tom. "The next time Jaki calls," I thought, "I'll be ready."

Outside My Window

*lives a world
new to me.
We fill a feeder
and birds
feast each day.
I sit beside it
and they
talk in trees,
"Can we trust
this intruder
who is not like us?"
I remember
the bird
on another patio
who'd visit
at lunchtime—
us hospital employees.
So safe was he
he'd eat from our hands.
I sit on my patio
while they talk in trees.
They fly quickly by
faster than clouds.
They touch perches
and leave
in a rush.
Soon they will know
they can trust
this intruder
who is not like us.*

The Temple Where Little Girls Worshipped

As far back as I can remember, I was enchanted by the precocious, talented, smiling personality of Shirley Temple. I had a blue cup made of glass which had her picture on it. I wouldn't drink my milk unless it was in my Shirley Temple cup. Her picture was barely visible after the many times my mother had washed my special cup for me. But that didn't matter to me. It had to be that cup.

A generation and a half later, it was with a mixture of feelings that I heard Shirley Temple Black would be visiting the auditorium of a company I worked for. After her talk I went to meet her. Her right hand was bandaged. As I began to briefly mention my childhood devotion to her, I became more concerned about her in the present and asked what happened to her hand. She laughed and told me how a huge Texan had told her what a fan of hers he was, as he crunched her small hand in his massive one. In his zeal it must have taken very little to give her a sprain. As she offered her left hand to me it seemed very small and vulnerable to me in my not so large hand.

I left the auditorium thinking about what someone had done to her. It was innocent. It was out of enthusiasm for her as a personality. I doubt she would remember our brief meeting. But I'm sure she remembers him.

WHEN BOBBY AND BOBBIE MADE MUSIC TOGETHER

*He touched the strings.
His bass fiddle responded
to his touch like I do.
The notes were gentle
waves of his own
sense of humor.
She said fitting sounds
back to him
on the keys.
Their music pleased
and teased everyone
the way it played itself
through their fingers.
They communicated
in unwritten jazz riffs
feeling the moment
filling the room
with creative delight,
none of it taped
just into the air
like a loving prayer.*

From the Bijou to Old Uncle Gaylord's

Five friends were sitting with us when one of them mentioned the movie. Each one had seen it and one of them planned to see it again. All of them recommended "From Mao To Mozart: Isaac Stern in China."

It was playing in Palo Alto at two theaters and nowhere else in the Bay Area. A week after the enthusiastic recommendation we had plans to be in Palo Alto again, so we went in early to see the film first.

"There are musicians and then there are musicians," to paraphrase my nephew, who teaches classical music. Isaac Stern is a <u>musician</u>. He demonstrated on his violin for the young Chinese students who aspired to play their best. His words were quickly translated for those who spoke no English. He needed no translation as, with humor, he strained and tugged at his violin, then looking the students deeply into their eyes, he said, "Open up. Play it like you feel it, like you want the music to be heard. The violin should feel as if it is another arm attached to you." Gently he coaxed and showed the way to play with feeling. When they tried it and it worked for them, he beamed his enthusiasm, "Very good!" as he put an encouraging arm around the one who dared to play from the heart.

The music, he said, was the instrument. It was the means for people to relate. As thousands in the hot auditorium fanned themselves, he made the instrument a living thing by what he brought out of it. In his exuberance he brought out that ability in the students who were eager to understand.

In humbleness and truth he concluded, "It is not the violin. It could be any instrument. It is the music. If you think that life cannot exist without music then you can become a musician."

People leaving the theatre in front of us called it a beautiful film. It was. It was so beautiful neither Bob nor I were ready for the words we knew would be there later on. We stepped out into the still hot evening and gradually began to talk about the feelings that had brought a lump to our throats and moisture to our eyes. When Isaac Stem taught by example, his face beatific in its smiling, open warmth, there was the spark—some call it love, some call it God—for anyone with eyes to see and anyone without, to feel.

We went into the Old Uncle Gaylord Ice Cream Parlor near the theatre. Standing at the counter making our important decision of which of the fresh and unadulterated flavors we would choose, we heard a woman's voice near the entryway.

"Are there any customers here?"

We turned around and saw an overweight, slightly disheveled woman, her short dark hair looking uncombed in the windless night.

She walked into the store slowly, her white cane in one hundred eighty degree sweeps of motion, like an erratic radar stick, hitting cane chairs in her path.

"We're here," we said

"Who are you?" she demanded.

"I'm Ruth. This is Bob,"

Bob said, "It's just the two of us,"

She came toward us.

Bob ordered our ice-cream sodas and we watched as he guided her verbally,

"Do you work here?" she asked him,

"No. I don't."

"Am I near the piano?"

"You're behind the piano, you have to walk out this way. Be careful of the sign."

"What does the sign say?" she asked quickly as she stepped away from it,

"Don't bump into me," Bob answered.

"Come on. What does it really say?" she insisted in her no nonsense voice. He read her the descriptions of the ice-cream dishes. She sat down at the piano and we turned back to the counter. A woman came into the store with a young boy. Her dress was in bright reds and white cotton, long, loose and embroidered with various colors of flowers near the neck. Her face was out of my distant past.

I said, "You look like my yoga teacher. Did you ever teach yoga?"

She said, "No. But I'm a teacher,"

"Where do you teach?"

"At Stanford,"

I was struck. Not my yoga teacher, yet I knew her.

I asked, "What do you teach?"

"Art History."

"You must be Bridgette. I took art history from you at the College of Marin!"

We invited her and her son to join us after they ordered. We took our sodas to the raised table in what was originally a display window, and began sipping their coolness,

The lady at the piano played something. She could play. We enjoyed her. Then she began singing, too. The piano was just an old upright, painted beige. The store had high ceilings and odd pieces of old furniture, some just old and funky, some of quality. Her voice was a surprise because our sight had fooled us. Her left bra strap, fallen midway down her arm remained there. Her hose in her Mary Jane shoes belied her age of maybe thirty. Her full contralto voice contained the pain of Piaf, the projection of Judy Garland, the boldness of her personality, and the beauty of Isaac Stern. It was a cultured, magnificent voice.

A man came in and sat. He wore a wool knitted pullover hat, a short sleeved shirt, shorts up to his groin and sneakers.

He asked her, "Do you know how to play, *It's Hard To Be Humble When You're Perfect In Every Way?*"

She said, "Sing it."

He sang the song once and she said in her firm way, "Sing it again."

He sang it again and she picked up the chords on the piano. When he was done, she repeated, "Sing it again." This time she sang it with him and played it, too.

While we were still laughing, his next question set into motion the swing of a mood, sudden as her cane had swung from left to right before.

"Do you know, *Lonely?*"

"How does it go?"

He began, once again, in his pleasant, clear voice, to sing words to her.

"I know that," she put her head almost on the keys of the piano, to her left and began to play. And when she sang *Lonely*—though hardly that, I felt the depth of loneliness.

While he taught her two other songs we talked with my former teacher, Bridgette, and her son who was almost five. Bridgette gave him some coins to put into a can on the piano bench. At first he didn't want to. She left them on the table and, smiling, gently said, "Maybe you'll decide you want to later." A little later they went over together to place the coins in the tip can.

When they came back Bridgette said, "We come here often and everytime we do they have all the furniture arranged differently." I thought about the singer.

Bob went over to give her some money and told her how George Shearing had announced his new album when we had heard him at the Marin Fair the week before, "The next number will be the title track of our latest album, *On A Clear Day I Still Can't See A Darn Thing.*"

Then she said, "Do you want me to play *On A Clear Day?*" Bob said, "Yes."

While she played it, Bridgette's son asked why they were giving the singer money.

His mother said, "That's how she makes her living."

Then Bob added, "That's also known as encouragement."

The boy asked, "What's that mean?"

Bob said, "I like what you're doing. Keep doing it."

The boy asked Bob, "How come you know so much?"

Bob smiled, "Because I've been around a long time—many lifetimes."

The boy accepted that.

The singer and the man finished the song she had just learned. She said, "Give him a hand. He's good."

Bridgette and her son had to leave. He had the promise of the slides at a park to go to. We had our appointment at eight, down the street. We looked at our watches. We looked into each other's eyes and we agreed we had time for two more songs.

A Poet Needs Words

*like thirsty earth
needs water;
no easier to find the poetry of
living when
life sears
and pain,
perceived as it is,
is swallowed whole
and melts hot inside.
We poets and non-poets
reach alike
to give
to love
to live the best we understand,
we poets and non-poets ...
We are all poets
of our own hearts.*

Office Visit

I stepped into the doctor's office. I was attracted to a framed message in calligraphy on the wall. I glanced at the various chairs and a couch and decided I would rather look at the rest of the wall hangings instead of sitting. There was a large, framed picture of a dog's face, looking down as one does in reading. This dog was wearing a pair of glasses. I wondered about the person who had been recommended to me to check my vision. First I had been offered words of wisdom, and then amusement, as I visualized the large brown and black dog reading better now that he'd had his eyes examined by the man I was about to meet.

The doctor opened the sliding opaque window and asked me some questions. He wrote my answers on a small white card and then showed me to the examination room. I don't know how much of an influence his artwork may have been; I felt a geniality about him. He had an easy manner. He seemed like a pleasant man, one who was at peace with his world.

As he began the exam he talked with me as though we were old friends. His speech was articulate without being pedantic. If I'd met him on a bus I would have perceived him as a learned man before he even spoke.

I viewed the eye chart across the room, stumbling on the hazy looking letters, guessing at them, as he gradually offered larger, darker print for me to read.

His name was a Russian name.

"I once had a Russian name," I said, "My maiden name."

He said, "I went to Russia two and a half years ago."

"My parents came from Kiev," I told him. "I was impressed, as a child, that they both came from Kiev, yet met in New York."

"I enjoyed Kiev best of all," he said. "It has lots of trees and hills. There is a river which runs and diverts, like this," he showed me, his hands parallel, then he spread his hands farther apart, "then it comes back together again."

He reflected on his travel memories, "It is a very beautiful city, more than Moscow or Leningrad." I had never heard of its beauty. I knew it only as the place my parents had left in order to survive.

His brilliant green eyes brightened even more, "Ninety percent of the employees work for the government. We were waiting for a train to go to Europe and I saw a pair of silver candlestick holders I was interested in. I asked the woman standing there if I could see them. She said, "No. I am on my break now." I said, "I would like to look at them, and offered her another ruble. "No, I will not give up my break."

"But I am an American, and I will be leaving on a train in two or three minutes." He smiled, "They are working for the government. They don't care."

He covered my right eye and asked me to tell him what I saw. "It's a blur."

He made a change, "Now?"

I read the letters, except for the last one.

He said, "Tea is only two or three cents for a big pot in Kiev. You can have all you want. Or at least it was that cheap two and a half years ago. But coffee," again his clear green eyes twinkled, "it costs twenty or thirty cents. But you can't get a second cup!"

I expressed surprise.

He said, "I asked the lady for another cup of coffee and she said, "I will have to see if it's all right,"

"And the cups are so small, like this." He held his fingers only two inches apart.

He continued, in his easy manner, examining my eyes. Then he stood back, "My family left the country in 1926. We lived closer to China, near the Yangtze River, so we moved to Manchuria."

"Did you learn to speak Chinese?"

"No, they all spoke Russian."

My doctor began to talk about his father who had been a doctor. He never said one word specifically of praise about his father. He just talked about the free clinic on Wednesdays his father had established because the people of his adopted country were so poor; about the children of widows he knew; about when they needed surgery and his father took them into his home. The doctor reminisced about his father. Clearly he loved him with the love of deep respect.

"I would come home from school," he said, "and my father would say we will be having this one or that one staying with us for the next couple of weeks, recuperating from surgery. It was an ongoing changing of people."

The doctor had talked about other countries he'd enjoyed, like England and Australia. In each case, there was someone he had talked with and had retained in his memory, to bring the country into closer focus.

My eyes had hardly changed. He said it was really up to me whether I wanted to have the prescription filled. I asked what he would do if it were his eyes. "I would get them, for a second pair, in case something happens to your other ones, when you're traveling."

Just before we parted, he said his father had practiced medicine for seventy years and never sent anyone a second bill. He said that if a patient could afford to pay the bill, he wanted to show respect by not sending a second one, and if a patient could not afford to pay he sent no second bill also out of respect.

I walked outside. Car headlights were coming on as dusk approached. I felt warmed as though I'd just walked into the sunlight.

Cool It

On a very hot day in July
Mel Torme wrote his hit song,
"Chestnuts Roasting on an Open Fire,"
a winter song,
a cool tune
from a cool cat.
It helps me appreciate
the measure of words
to be immeasurable.
We can think ourselves
into and out of
just about anything
we can imagine.

Imagine that!

I Think His Name Was Hans

This happened on a small Greek ship, going to Puerto Vallarta. It was my first cruise, other than a few hours of an afternoon, and I was wide-eyed with excitement.

I hadn't thought about Hans, or the incident, until twelve years later, when planning a cruise with my husband. I was single on the first trip, traveling alone for the first time.

I met Hans at dinner. He was a very small man, short, and far from handsome. He, too, was traveling alone. His personality struck a chord in fellow travelers that brought laughter, at his expense, whenever we sat together. He talked about himself, as many are prone to do. People didn't believe him. They saw him as the runt in the litter and denied his being. I listened to him and searched his eyes. He was just another human being, no more, no less. With hardly any words, I assured him I knew that.

At first, optimistically, I waited to see if the others would get bored with their derision. We were on a pleasure craft, in winter, heading for the warm sun. But, no matter how they may have left their personal problems behind, here, in Hans, was their immediate scapegoat. Whether he was aware or just didn't care, I can't say. He came back each time anyway.

I thought that everyone aboard was going to disembark in Puerto Vallarta. About the third day of our journey I learned that the people I met were returning home once we reached Puerto Vallarta.

My destination became very important to those who were going home sooner.

"My travel agent didn't tell me I could do that," said one.

Someone else said, "Wait until I get a hold of my travel agent."

Some people seemed happy for me to be going on, when Puerto Vallarta was the turning point for them. To their questions I enthused, "After that, I'm flying to Guadalajara, then to Guanajuato by limousine and on to San Miguel de Allende ... "

They interrupted in their enthusiasm, "That's the artist colony!"

"Yes, so I hear. I'm looking forward to it."

"Then where do you go?"

"On to Mexico City; after a couple of nights there, I fly home."

"You'll love Mexico City. They call it 'Mexico.' While you're traveling you'll meet people who are coming from the places you are going to. They'll tell you the best places to eat and everything. You'll have a wonderful time."

Hans seemed quieter than usual, and just listened. And then, on the fourth day, the day before I would be leaving, Hans announced, "Everyone meet at midnight by the pool tonight. I am hosting a farewell party for Ruth."

This was the Hans that no one believed.

"He'll never do it. He's too tight," said one.

"Another likely story," said another.

As I said, it was a small ship, made to hold about two hundred passengers. There was no doubt about the pool site. There was only one little swimming pool. As I dressed in my cabin that evening, I wondered if any guests would arrive.

I walked to the pool. There was Hans, my thoughtful host, seeing to the flow of champagne as everyone arrived, just in case.

Lady of the Birds
(For Jen Ewing)

She holds doors for me as I trundle through
with overflowing groceries.
A light rap later at my door,
she invites me to tea
that afternoon.
I make friends
when thoughts are far and people near
responding to something that I am.
I take my book of poetry
place it wrapped in her hands.
Unusual for me to do that
with someone I've just met.
But she has a smile, which opens doors of generosity.
I feel like I have entered a bright passage
as I visit with her and family.
Birds seem to know
her patio is their sanctuary.
They rush to feed
to linger, to live there
among the many hanging hide-outs
she's provided.
Like wind at sea, as one they fly
beyond our vision.
The sleeping cat
so warm and satisfied
has not disturbed his dreams.
The birds, as one again,
return as fast as they had gone,
to feed, to linger, to live there
among the many hanging hide-outs
provided by
the lady of the birds.

Where's Your Peacock?

I was sitting in a churchyard in the sun. A little girl, just out of class, walked by with her girlfriend and asked me, "Where's your peacock?"

I said, "Why did you ask me that?"

She kept walking and called over her shoulder, just as they were about to turn the corner of the old stone church, "I don't know. I thought you had a peacock."

I'm not sure why that question made me feel so good. I wondered if the girl mistook me for someone she'd once met who had a peacock. I used to be mistaken for Gogi Grant's sister, when I lived in the Mohave Desert. Once, in a local store, the owner began speaking to me, then he said, "But your hair is longer, and she usually comes in here in her bathing suit." Compared to her I must have looked formally dressed in my shorts.

"Maybe," I thought, "The girl asking about the peacock was trying to be funny." But that seemed like a sophisticated line of humor. No telling. The world is more sophisticated now than when I was her age. She was maybe nine or ten, about my oldest grandson's age.

Hearing her ask about my peacock took me back about a hundred miles north of San Francisco to a ranch.

My yoga teacher had arranged the trip for her students. We would have vegetarian meals, do yoga and meditate for the whole weekend.

We drove north and turned in to the secluded area that led us there. As we parked and stepped out to walk the few hundred yards to our destination I felt the cares of the world slide off my shoulders. There was a lot of greenery, so high we couldn't see anything else but that and sky. We passed between tall shrubs and trees to either side of us. There, ahead of us, lay a low Mexican style tile roofed structure which was the long dining room and huge kitchen. To its left were the sleeping cottages, ready for our needs.

Our weekend was more satisfying than I had expected. I found myself talking to the owner of this haven and sharing with her my hope to be hired for a job for which I'd applied near home. It was to be housemother to six special young ladies. Patty was a good and encouraging listener. She offered to give her reference. By the time we were ready to leave, she invited me up for another weekend. She was having a well-known doctor speak, and said, "Come up. I think you'll enjoy him."

Her charge for our weekend had been minimal, but I knew what she usually charged.

I didn't want her to think I wasn't interested, but I couldn't afford it, so I told her the truth.

She said, "I don't want you to pay. You can help me get the food ready. Won't you come up?"

I gratefully accepted.

The Friday of the planned weekend, I drove there after work, went straight to the kitchen, and asked Patty very seriously what I should do.

She said, "Why don't you go for a swim before dinner. Everything's almost ready."

Dinner was for about twenty-five people. I'd have the swim, I thought, and help wash dishes later. There were two sinks; I'd use one of them.

Immediately after dinner, I went into the kitchen to wash dishes. Patty was there, "Why don't you listen to the speaker and tell me what he said. I have plenty of help with my daughters here."

I dutifully went and listened to the speaker under the holy stars winking at one another.

"I must remember everything he said," I thought, as I found an empty chair up front.

Patty and I talked later. I was prepared to tell her what she'd missed, like a book report. She began talking about herself. "I'm a

Leo," she said, "A leader, and all my life I've had everything without doing anything for it. I wanted to work and do things for others." She paused, and then said, "My father built this ranch many years ago. He loved Mexico so much he brought home as much of it as he could. That's why there are so many artifacts all over the place from that country."

She seemed so content after cooking and cleaning up in the kitchen, this lady who had a mansion in town, as well. There wasn't a bit of pretension in her, and she wasn't about to allow any in.

My eyes were getting heavy with the late hour. Half awake, I listened to her low voice and the high wail of her peacocks in the distance.

Perhaps that's part of why I felt so good when that little girl said, "I don't know. I thought you had a peacock."

How Ruth Felt

I'm curled up in bed
under the fluffiest eggplant colored quilt
listening to the mellowest jazz
reading Obama's "Dreams From My Father"
when a title comes up on
the Real Jazz Channel:
"How Ruth Felt," played by
Regina Carter.
I'm inside my peaceful side
and hear a song I'd never heard
and I've been digging jazz for sixty years.
It's got to be the title for all of me.
I've been writing memoirs
before I knew the meaning
of the word.
Thanks. I'll accept that one.
I'm inside and
I trust and love it there,
the part of me that shivers
when I hear truth
that covets petting my silky cat.
I harass him more with my touch
when he'd rather sleep
than he could ever irritate me
even when knocking fragiles to the floor.
How Ruth felt - inside and out.
I feel the meaning of
all there is and isn't
lying under the fluffiest eggplant colored quilt.

Savoring

George Santos lived across the road from me. His land and house were that much closer to the mountain.

When I first met him he may have been about forty, but he always seemed like an older man to me. It was his memories, which, spotted here and there, between other words, made him seem old. And, too, he had a politeness like a man of other generations would. Tall and slim, it seemed like he almost always wore the same cap, shirt and pants whenever we saw each other in front of the house. The cap, he always reached toward, as though to tip. From working with his vegetables, cap, shirt and pants looked all the same, khaki blended with good earth, and always suspenders were a part of his outfit.

He had a lot to say about small animals and vegetables, about fruit trees and the land. There were six fruit trees growing in my front yard. Before I moved in, they had grown wild and unattended until the pear tree near the front door grew a branch which swooped almost to the ground. I took a saw to it to save anyone from tripping on this misshapen tree. In my zeal and ignorance, I took off almost half the tree. That's how I met George. He came by, offering the way to seal the branch so the tree would live. From time to time he would wander by. I'd see him from the picture window, making sure the tree was doing all right. The next time we met he said,

"I think it's going to make it."

George lived alone across the road from me. He'd lived there all his life. He would tell me with pride how years ago his father and uncle owned the entire hill. How mountain cats would come down the mountain to feed. Now there was only an occasional deer.

"In the old days this hill was full of deer," he seemed to be there in those days as he shared his memories. He would assure me that no "big shots" would be able to put up any high rise on his land and take away my view of Mount Tamalpais.

George was at home most of the time, released from the army with a pension and a chronic stomach ailment. He raised a few chickens and cared for his garden. When the fava beans were ready for picking he brought them over. When the herring were running on one certain day in Sausalito, all the neighbors who wanted it had herring.

George loved my grey-striped cat. The cat would sit on George's wooden fence by the hour, he told me, ready for the hunt. George said, with devotion, "That cat looks like those wild mountain cats that used to come around here, but they're all gone now. He's a great little hunter, your cat."

One day George told me how he had acquired an increasing number of small life. He said that when people bought their kids pets, like for Easter, and then the kids didn't take care of them, the parents would drive by and toss them over his fence because they knew he would take care of them. So, little by little, George had a variety of small life to nurture.

Considering that I lived there for about ten years, I didn't see George many times, but each time was with a feeling of respect, a sharing of information about the important things, and his deep sense of nostalgia.

When I thought it was time to move away, he wandered by one last time. I reached into the storage room for my old fishing bag and my best rod and reel and gave them to George.

It took me eight years to go back up that hill. Eight years of growth and change. When I finally did visit my good neighbor and introduced him to my husband, it was with a kaleidoscope of feelings as I looked across the road at a house I had left—but not completely. The house, with additions and sparkling new paint, had, too, grown and changed. And I said goodbye to it, as I had never done in legal or mental form before. Another cycle of eight closed for me, as I stopped looking back and began a new one.

I didn't know if George Santos would recognize me after all those years and arriving unexpectedly. I expected him to be somewhere outside, either loving his garden or his banties in his unique way. We opened the old wooden gate door which swung wide enough to admit a truck, and as I walked onto his piece of land I knew it was still the same as it must have been in years past when he walked up from the incline to talk about land and living things to me. The foliage along the road was so dense and so tall I never had seen beyond it. He was nowhere about. A few moments passed and someone turned up the dirt road rise, coming in from the street down below. He said George was right out in the back, behind the barn, working on his truck.

We walked around to the back of the barn and saw him. He wore his cap, as always, his bright red suspenders and khaki clothes. As we approached I asked, "George, do you remember me?" He looked at Bob and took a long, careful look at me. "Sure I do;" he said my name.

He warmed up to Bob quite quickly, which pleased us both more than it ordinarily might, with someone else, because George created a quiet, country world for himself, with life's simplest pleasures and few people.

We had brought up the little story I'd written about him, to share. His eyes, he said, weren't so good; Bob read him the words. I watched George's face. He was sitting beside me on a bench by the barn, savoring each memory. When Bob paused, George said, "That's right. How did you remember that? I almost forgot that myself." Then when Bob finished, George said, "I want a copy to give to my sister."

As though that were a passport to lead us back in time. George invited us into his house, telling us as we walked what each plant and each tree was. He said his house was old and not fixed up. He was in tune with it exactly as it was. He only wanted to prepare us for its difference. We walked inside and with one step both felt transported back a hundred years. In great surprise, beyond the wood burning stove, I saw and asked, "What's that T.V. doing here?" Large, heavy framed photos of men who were his uncle and his father looked out from the green wooden walls. A true host in his castle, he asked us to sit down. I chose the rocker, from which George cleared stacks of newspapers. He began to talk about the hill where he lives, and the surrounding towns, as they were around the turn of the century. He repeated the things that had been repeated to him about family and communities the generation before.

He said, "If you're interested, I could show you some albums of what it was like in the old days."

We shared them between our laps as George recalled and reminisced. I thought the local library would appreciate the value of those photos and George assured me, "Oh, yeah. My niece, she took them over there once."

When he served us some fresh sweetened blackberries that grew wild on his land, he gave generously and made sure we had paper napkins. When he told one story after another of times he would never see again, and some of times he never did, he spoke as they did then, his head to the side a bit, his eyes looking skyward, his tongue barely meeting the comer of his mouth.

I left with special memories of a man I understood, after our brief visit, more than I had in the many years we had been neighbors.

Knowing

*I don't know
where life leads
its infinitesimal
diamond-like facets.*

*A long life ago
I knew
more than I do now.*

*Beyond comprehension, I expanded in moments
to being at one with vastness of all
in the galaxy.*

*No sooner that explosion of consciousness
and I was at one again,
this time smaller than
the smallest atom.*

*Only ten
I kept this to myself
for seven years.*

*Now, almost eight times more
I can't say I know.*

*According to the Bard of Avon,
There are more things
in heaven and earth, Horatio
than are dreamt of
in your philosophy.
This I know.*

Trusting

No one ever felt like I was a threat. I attracted people who needed someone to talk with about their lives and problems. At first there was a subtlety I didn't recognize because of my own depression.

I was alone in the private company garden trying to let the beauty of flowers surrounding me still my anxieties. When I slowed my breathing and focused on one part of nature it did help.

A woman I'd never met sat near me. With only a half hour lunch, she zeroed in on her problems and, in a few minutes, revealed her troubles to me. While I listened, I wondered why Kim had selected me. I felt the magnitude of responsibility. My quiet manner, sincere caring, the way my own dark, sad eyes explored the blue of Kim's, there was immediate bonding on a higher level. It was as if Kim knew that I was a person she could tell her innermost feelings to, even though we'd never met before.

That was the first time. The warm, sunny day stayed in my mind, the sculpted lawn with shade trees, and the paths that led only to concrete commercial matters.

The next time, I was at work. I had to go to Carol's desk for some forms. We spoke a few friendly words and I mentioned, "I live in Mill Valley." I didn't know why I said it. It was unlike me to initiate. I prided myself on being a good listener. Saying more than I had to say, more than people expected me to say, made me feel like I was telling a secret I wasn't supposed to tell. It made me feel vulnerable, emotionally unclothed.

Carol didn't seem to notice. She said, "I heard it's beautiful there."

"Haven't you ever been to Mill Valley?"

"I've never been out of San Francisco—except once, when I was a child, I was in San Jose."

"Why? How come you never leave San Francisco?"

"I've never told this to anyone else before."

I looked intently at Carol.

"...I can tell you," she paused again, "...I'm afraid to go anywhere outside the city."

"That's all right. You don't have to." Someone else was trusting me again with their deepest fear, not seeing mine, knowing it was safe to tell me.

Carol visibly relaxed. I kept talking. I didn't know what I was going to say before it came out of me. I only knew I had to say the things that Carol needed to hear.

"I think I understand," I heard myself say. Carol smiled weakly. "No one else does when I make excuses why I won't go anywhere."

"You're able to go to work."

"Yes, but that's still in the city"

I gambled, "Would you like to see my house. It's beautiful in Mill Valley."

"I want to, but I can't go over the bridge."

I touched Carol's shoulder, "You can't, .. or you won't?"

"You're right. I wish I could go, but... "

"You don't have to be afraid to go with me. But it's up to you."

I watched Carol's eyes. "I have to get back to my desk. I'll come see you after work and see what you decided. We can have dinner at my house."

Carol watched as I walked between the rows of desks toward the claims department.

At four-thirty I went to see Carol. She was putting papers away, preparing to leave. When she opened the bottom drawer of the desk and took out her purse she looked up and saw me smiling.

"You want me to go with you, don't you?"

I knew what I would say. "I do, but I won't try to convince you. If you decide to go and want to go back, I'll turn around anytime you say,"

Carol looked at me for a lifetime.

"I'm going to go with you, but I won't stay for dinner."

"I'm glad you decided to do it. If you change your mind about dinner I'd like that."

We talked on the ride north. I assured Carol during the trip, in every way I could. I gave confidence I didn't have for myself. My lacking didn't detract. I was a calming influence, so that by the time we approached the bridge, Carol could have been any of the thousands of commuters who daily crossed the Golden Gate Bridge. When I couldn't think of anything further to say, I glanced to my right to see how Carol was doing.

"I'm OK," Carol said, surprised at her bravado. "I'm actually crossing the bridge and leaving the city!"

I heaved a sigh of relief—for now. What if Carol panicked? What could I do?

By the time we had crossed over the water, we were both exultant.

"This is like a miracle. Thank you, Ruth, for what you did for me."

"Thank you for trusting me."

We drove quietly for the next ten minutes, each of us marveling and savoring inwardly.

"You're right," Carol said, as we pulled into the driveway. "It is very beautiful in Mill Valley,"

"Come in. I'll show you my house."

Carol liked the unique house with its sunken living room and various nooks and crannies. We sat on the sofa looking at Mt. Tamalpais and the way fog curled around the reclining Indian princess, and moved like shadow dancers.

"I want to go back now."

"...OK—no dinner first?"

"No. I want to go back now,"

"I'll take you back, just like I promised."

The ride back was easier for both of us. Carol knew she could do it.

Cadence

*They come,
generations,
leaving footprints in the sand,*

*generations
of expanding consciousness,*

*making imprints,
leaving patterns
weaving messages
beyond their own
conscious comprehension.*

*They come,
anointing the way
to expanding consciousness
like a silent garden
growing lush
through life
for new generations.*

Pianta

Pianta had been in America from the old country for so many years. But he remembered his youth like it was that very morning. He was the first born of twelve. He herded goats in light of dawn to the valley behind the house, where they fed on thick green carpets of dewy grass. Pianta ate his chunk of cheese and bread, swished it down with the bottle of half wine, half water his father prepared for him. He dreamed of coming to America as he watched the animals under his care. Bells hanging around their necks tinkled in harmony as they bent and moved from spot to spot in the verdant valley.

Pianta was small. His body grew strong and healthy as he helped with everything his father did. Lifting forks of hay high over his head for hours in the sun browned his skin and made his muscles wiry.

Pianta never let go of his dream to live in America. When most of his brothers and sisters were old enough to help, he received the chance.

Uncle Georgio wanted an apprentice. He wrote a letter to Pianta's father, "Dear Brother, My business is growing quickly and I need help. In this country the young boys are not serious. They are still children. I will teach your oldest son how to be a cooper. He can live with me till he gets some money saved. If you say yes, I will send you enough money for his boat trip and enough for you to make it worthwhile for you to let go of your oldest. Pianta can pay me back for the boat trip after his apprenticeship is finished, and I begin paying him. Dear brother, this is truly the land of opportunity. I hope you will help me at the same time you give your son a chance. I send my love to you and your family, Georgio."

When Pianta read the letter to his parents he jumped for joy, "Papa, can I go, Papa! Will you let me?"

"Pianta, I have to think about it. I never saw you so excited..."

"Yes, Papa, that is my dream...to go to America."

"I didn't know."

"Papa, when I come home with the goats, I make believe I am coming home in the country where Uncle Georgio lives."

"Why, Pianta—why do you want to leave your family that loves you?"

"Papa—Momma—that is the only part I don't like. I love you. I will miss you. But I want to learn the ways of the new world."

So it was that Pianta went to America when he was sixteen.

Hard as the work was till then, Pianta worked twice as hard for his uncle. He missed the bells of grazing goats who lazed the start of day with him. The only bells he heard anymore were to signal the start and end of each workday, twelve, fourteen hours apart. Pianta paled in the dark distillery, making barrels, and though he was physically strong, by the time his apprenticeship was over, his spirits were weakened.

Maria had a room in the same boarding house as Pianta. She was not only the most beautiful woman he had seen since he'd come to America, and smart, she also came from the southern part of his country.

Her skin was pure white. Her black eyes followed Pianta's every motion. He moved his hands rapidly when he spoke and Maria's eyes danced with his fingers. Neither of them had very much money. She worked as a clerk selling ladies' hats. He had moved from his uncle's place soon as he could save enough for rent. Both of them sent what they could back home.

When work was finished, Pianta and Maria walked together, holding hands, making plans for their future.

They found a small house where rent was a little more than they had both paid at the boarding house. Pasta and soup were hearty and cheap.

When children came along, Pianta became the sole breadwinner. He had two jobs. He knew about hard work. It was nothing new to him.

Maria, his growing family, and the ones in the old country, were the world to Pianta.

He never stopped helping. Pianta wanted his parents to come to America, but they didn't want to change their lives. They died, one after the other, never having left their village.

Maria and Pianta had eight children. It was always a struggle to get by. But Maria was careful with Pianta's hard earned money. Pianta never allowed himself sickness. When he became too old to be a cooper, well into his seventies, when speed was what a young boss wanted from him, Pianta felt lucky to stay on as a packer.

One night Pianta's grandfather came to him in a dream and said, "You've had a hard life, so I'm going to give you the winning lottery number."

Pianta used to play the Chinese lottery, but never won.

He went early the next morning, the number embedded in his mind, and played it.

Pianta won more money than he had ever seen in all his life, more than he would need if he lived to be one hundred fifty.

He kept working. And when he went to sleep each night, he heard the harmony of bells dangling around the necks of grazing goats.

A Song for My Daughter

I'd heard of Charlotte.
We met tonight, on the phone.
She, who cannot see,
I felt the aura of blindness not to see her.

Do I have a favorite song or does my daughter?
There are so many that not one comes to mind.
Charlotte will be singing at the Plaza
the place with an elegant name
that houses ebbing lives, the place where Riki lives
attached to life by a cord.

Of course there is a song, the one Riki wrote to me
just before I flew to Mexico, so long ago,
Stevie Wonder's "You are the sunshine of my life.
That's why I'll always be around."
I woke one day in Mexico and knew I'd not return to
California until I went back East to Riki.
How could I know, with that choice
I was opening a door
I'd closed long before
when I divorced her dad?
"You are the sunshine of my life."
Through Riki's love
my idea of visiting two weeks became a turning point,
in which I stayed two years, remarried to her dad
before we returned to California

"A capella" Charlotte sang to me on the phone.
With my request she will sing a song
for my daughter at the Plaza,
Charlotte, who sings like an angel and cannot see
to Riki who loves like an angel who can barely speak.

The Quiet One

My pen became my best friend soon as I learned to write. I felt comfort between my fingers no one could ever take away with spoken words that paralyzed my throat. In school, when I was eight years old, poetry became my voice as I wrote and tried to listen to my teacher at the same time.

In spite of my solitary life where daydreams blocked out words that filled the classroom, I was considered a good, though timid, student. Throughout school years I managed to get excellent grades. Not by anything I said, but from my written tests and compositions.

I loved words. When classmates groaned at their assignments, I was always secretly happy to write a story for homework. But my love for writing was overshadowed by trepidation which leeched that happiness. Each morning I looked forward to school, to learning from my teacher. Dread would gradually seep into my consciousness like an insidious disease, catching my breath away, making my throat a tight vise of apprehension. By the time I reached school, which was only three houses away, I was pale and breathless, afraid I would have to talk.

Rarely was I called upon to stand up and recite. But everyday I feared I would be called to speak in front of thirty others. Once I heard a classmate tell another, after an oral report, "I was so scared my knees were shaking." I wished harder than I'd ever wished for anything before that I could hide terror beneath my skirt where no one could see. When I spoke, my voice choked and rose to a higher pitch. It lost its resonance. I talked haltingly, as though asking permission for every syllable that was about to leave my quivering lips. I felt no assurance as words hopped out like cackling geese and faces showed no feeling. My throat was seized with dry pain.

One day the eighth grade class was told to expect the principal. Mrs. Palmer was going to visit for a very special reason and the class would sing together while Mrs. Palmer listened.

I heard my own voice as I sang with the class. Mrs. Palmer walked slowly up and down the narrow aisles, putting her head next to someone, and then she would walk a few feet and stoop to listen to someone else.

Everyone tried to watch where she was, without squirming too much. She was behind me before I knew it. Her left ear almost touched my mouth. "You have a beautiful contralto voice."

Mrs. Palmer walked to the front of the class. She and the teacher whispered while most of the class whispered to each other. But not I. I tried to hear what was being said by the two, but the noise of the many drowned it out.

After school I ran home and looked up the meaning of contralto.

The next day I learned I had been selected to sing solo at graduation. The thrill of this was the most exciting thing I had ever experienced. For a few minutes I forgot. Then my joy was dulled by sickening fear. I thought of not singing. But knew that I would. I would do it. I wanted to. I couldn't imagine saying no to my teacher and the principal. Rehearsals were after school. Mrs. Palmer made sure I would remember to smile by instructing the class to applaud anytime I didn't. Mrs. Palmer faced the back of the room, listening for my contralto, and for applause.

When the class applauded, Mrs. Palmer said, "Start at the beginning, Ruth, and smile while you sing, so the class doesn't applaud till you've finished the song." I learned the words, and after a few rounds of premature applause, learned to smile throughout the song.

On graduation night, seeing the line up of my classmates wearing caps and black gowns, in the darkly lit area back stage, was an Ingmar Bergman movie reeling into my deepest fear. Voice cracking, I sang. *There's a happy land somewhere, and it's just a prayer away.* Though my voice was shaky, as I always knew it, straining to come out, to be heard, the only applause was when I finished.

In college I took every creative writing class available. They gave my soulful voice a chance to say the thoughts that came through me on paper. One of my classes was in a round room. Instead of desks and chairs, the room was made of circular graduated steps that were carpeted. Its symbolism of wholeness and life deeply affected me. In that room I read my poems, starting out shaky and nervous, like I had always done. I looked up as I read, seeing enthusiasm and interest in the eyes of others. That helped. I remembered to take breaths. My voice sounded good!

One day one of the students, who had a video camera from another class, took footage of me while I read. We watched the playback. Once again I realized—I have a pretty voice.

When the college's first annual poetry conference was being planned, I felt encouraged to read my poetry. Yevtushenko was on the program as honored guest and would read in Russian with a translator; Jessamyn West was scheduled to talk. And I, to a smaller audience, in a room of two hundred people, read my poetry proudly, courageously, with feeling.

It was as though a dam had broken. A lifetime of suppressed feelings rushed out. I felt free. This single change made me happy for the first time in my life. Friendships felt closer. I wrote because I love to write, not as a substitute for speaking. Speaking was of such great proportion to me that my talking became compulsive. Where once I listened, now I talked, until my closest friends said, "I don't want to hear it. That's enough,"

I asked for a ride to class with my teacher, Jeff, and his wife, Teresa. Jeff became friends with his students. In fact, Teresa was his student before she was his wife. She proposed to Jeff. My car was in the mechanic's shop. Jeff and Teresa lived down the street from me.

Jeff was bluntly honest, "We want a quiet morning. You can ride with us if you promise not to talk. I don't think you can do it."

My life flashed before me like some experience on dying. I saw the years of anguish, suppression and embarrassment; for my feelings of inadequacy, the times I didn't say what I wanted to express because of fear. I laughed at the irony, "OK. I promise not to talk. I can do it."

Sitting in the back seat behind Teresa, I was surprised at how quiet they were. Outside of an occasional comment, neither Jeff nor Teresa spoke much. It was the commute hour. Traffic was moving well. We should be at the first class of the day in about half an hour. Once in awhile Jeff spoke to Teresa and would include me, I nodded in response. Jeff saw me in the rear view mirror.

The sickening sound, sudden and violent, as tons of metal hit each other, tore into our consciousness. Two cars in the fast lane barely missed us as they collided with each other, nightmare of sight and sound. Teresa thought their small car was hit, and screamed, "Oh, my God, we could have been killed."

The two cars were still spinning like a gyroscope let loose, smoke screening their tangled bodies. Jeff followed the slowed trafflc as drivers craned to see through the thickening smoke. His voice was nervous as he said to Teresa, "Calm down. You're shaking. The highway patrol will be here soon. And we're safe."

"I can still hear that horrible crash in my head," she said, tears on her cheeks. He put his arm around Teresa, and then as if he just remembered, glanced back at me, and said, "Why didn't you say something?"

I, in a calm, clear voice, said, "But I promised not to say a word."

One Morning

For a split of a second
I believe I knew
how Helen Keller
may have felt
the first time meaning absorbed her
beyond unhearing ears
unspeaking voice.

This knowing came about
in simplicity, as wonders often do.

As was his almost daily habit
our cat jumped onto my bed,
onto my chest,
this time my sleeping chest
because, unlike typical timing
I'd begun to write at midnight
the night before.
In a few minutes he stood and
as he often does
showed great interest
in the trappings of my tall étagère
that I use as a headboard,
its alcove filled with things
no cat should dare:
a basket of catch-alls, papers and books
once my mother-in-law's
rose painted porcelain lamp
the phone right beside it
both on a square inverted rattan box
a soft leather case

*for my glasses
a rose colored holder
of too many pencils and pens
a basket of snacks
a control for warming the bed
a non-working pen
with a rose at its end
sitting in a wicker candle holder
the candle mostly spent
and a row of four necklace holders
opened by lifting their lids.*

*True, no cat should dare.
But this one, after his morning visit
stands and purposefully
walks to the étagère.
I dread to think his actually arriving there.
I intervene each time.*

*For once I waited
watched to see
what he would do.
He didn't go there
though he looked intent.
Instead he sat, placed silky furred head
at nape of my neck and stayed.*

*I believe I DO know
how Helen Keller
may have felt
the first time
meaning absorbed her
beyond unhearing ears
unspeaking voice.*

*Our cat being a cat
did what he always does.
The magnified sound of his purring
directly into my ear
was like hearing
for the first time.
The funny little sounds that followed
were undoubtedly his snoring.*

*My morning bodily needs
could even wait especially when
a jarring noise
like a mass of snow falling off the roof
startled us as one,
and neither of us moved.*

St. Michael's Waiting Room

I raised the cup of tea to my lips and sipped while I listened. Then I lifted the small heavy iron pot and added a little more to my cup, leaving the rest in the pot to keep it hot. I felt as though I were in Europe in a small, out of the way coffee house, maybe Paris. My eyes, like a child's, observed the crystal chandelier, the painting of abstracts and nudes on the walls. The people around me added to my feeling of ambience. They were a mixture of types and personalities, a blend of ages. I might have been anywhere. My imagination flew with the chords I was listening to. I pretended I was someplace in Europe. Students sat drinking espresso, eating scones, others having pastries which were piled with mounds of whipped cream, and made in the kitchen in back. I looked around, enjoying the sight of students who came to write and study. Two of them were sketching the musicians in charcoal. My eyes took in the huge healthy fern above the glass refrigerated case.

This room, warm with laughter and voices in quiet conversation, was the local meeting place in Palo Alto. The owner, a medium-built man in his middle fifties, was ruddy, graying and always there with kind of a twinkle in his bright, alert eyes, which were magnified by his glasses, and a sense of humor that was more sensed than spoken. He looked as though he was invited to a surprise party and had arrived with a gift, only to learn that the party had been given for him.

I had been there almost weekly since I'd noticed the place. There were always good musicians; people who loved to play. The first time I walked in was a cold, damp night, the kind in summer that people from other states discover too late when they come to vacation.

This evening there was a singer named Ida performing with a small group. She sang, her rusty toned long hair, bright in the light of a crystal wall sconce to each side of her. Her full skirted dress and vest looked Tyrolienne. Her cheeks, rosy with excitement and enthusiasm, were raised and full from her wide open smile. Outside of that intimate room and maybe some parts of the Bay Area, Ida, walking down a street, would have been recognized only by her expression of contentment, her look of trust, if anyone looked closely enough beyond her voluptuous body.

A little girl was there. She was sitting at the table to the left of the bandstand, where Ida sat. When Ida sang, the girl went to the bass player and, fetchingly said a few words. He raised her to his lap, and without missing a single note, held her as he played.

I watched the little girl across the room, who soon got down and visited people at one of the tables. She looked about four years old. The girl had a single daisy in her hand. She returned to stand in front of the combo, holding the flower in both hands, like a bride might do. From time to time she spoke to the bass player and he gave her his attention, as he plucked and moved his rapid fingers. Ida sang with sincerity like a child, sometimes like a flute, other songs coquettish. If fame had found her she could be no better. The room was her kingdom; her voice her magic wand. The little girl continued moving about, going from one table to another, stopping at each table a moment or two. Every table had a small ceramic vase filled with different kinds of fresh flowers. As she left each one, another flower was added to her hands. She returned to stand in front of the combo again while they played, holding her growing bouquet in both hands, as she had done before with a single flower. She stood quite still, as though posing for a five minute sketch. Then her four year old momentum carried her to another table, to another flower, until her bouquet had grown larger than any in the room.

She finally reached me. Her blue and white printed dress was a dainty design. She asked, "Do you have a dress on?"

"No. It's a blouse. I'm wearing pants."

The girl bent down and looked under the table to confirm what she had heard. She stood, adjusted her large bouquet of short stemmed flowers, and as in one motion, reached and asked if she could have the flowers at my table.

"You may have one. Which one do you want?"

The girl hesitated, but not for very long, then took her choice and went to the next table. The couple there soon had an empty vase. The woman said, "Aren't you going to leave any for us?" The little girl considered seriously, and with a sly grin, put some back. The woman smiled, and the girl quickly reached and took all but one.

I reached for my white angora hat. When I'd come in, the owner was wearing his black bowler, standing where he usually liked to stand, at the far corner of the counter. He had greeted me, admiring my hat with delight. Now I saw the bowler upright on a little table near the door. He, with his silent humor, and his glass of white wine, was in his same spot, only this time with one of the musician's straw hats covering his thinning hair. I stood, reluctant as always, to leave the mood created there. The little girl's energy, seemingly endless, carried her back to the tables she had visited before. Each time she added yet another flower to her growing bouquet. I stood and waved to the owner, almost with a tip of my hat, one to the other, till the next time.

The Kiss

*We met once before
in the park.
He was colorful and
drew attention
with his exotic ways.
Months passed before
we met again.
He seemed at home
in our home.
Before I knew
he kissed me,
the first kiss
I ever had
from a handsome
single macaw.*

The Vase

Mary was always ready with a hug, excited to see and be with the people in her life. "I like Christmas," she smiled. "I'm going to buy you a present in the store for Christmas," she grinned and jumped up and down like she'd done for almost twenty years, clapping her hands, drooling a little as she leaned to hug her happiness at the thought.

I thanked her but was concerned that Mary would use money for staff that was intended for her devoted family.

I saw and felt her pure egoless love as direct as any angel's must be. I didn't want her innocence to get her into trouble with family plans for a shopping list. Each day when she talked about her upcoming trip to the store to buy me a present, Mary shivered in delight. Her large eyes were shinier and browner than ever.

A memo arrived about the Christmas store. It would be open for three days so students could go shopping. A classroom down the hall was set up. PTA members were there to help with the sale of gifts that had been donated and collected all year. They read the students' gift lists, gift wrapped their choices and checked off the names. For two or three dollars total, a whole family could be shopped for at the twenty-five cent, fifty cent and one dollar tables. Silver trays, exotic perfumes, and pen and pencil sets were bought and wrapped.

Mary's class didn't get their shopping time until the second day. Mary fluctuated between her usual behavior and a dreamy look of anticipation for her turn.

When she got her chance, Mary went as if she were being selected to receive the Pulitzer Prize. She came back with a glow about her, tousled hair surrounding her not quite pretty face. It didn't matter at all what she had selected. It didn't matter that she was unaware of herself in the way that—in most of us—just gets in the way.

"I got this for you," she said, as she handed me the gift she'd been dreaming of finding. Her hug was more like the meaning of life than any I had ever known before.

I carefully opened the PTA wrapped package. Mary rubbed her hands together in suspense and excitement. "I hope you like it!"

The white tapered vase was not quite six inches tall. It had two opened porcelain roses and above them a pink rosebud. Above them were two more buds; these were white. The pale green leaves touched with veins of gold curved on their way up stems that looked like a single stem nurturing, supporting the white and pink flowers. Under the flowers were diamond shaped openings, as though they formed a trellis. The back of the vase had the same trellis-like design, which were both circled in lines of gold.

Mary had chosen as her gift: herself, the delicate, fragile vessel, uniquely lovely for its essence. It didn't matter that the filigree beauty of the vase prevented it from being able to contain water. The vase, as Mary, was perfect, just the way it was.

Extraordinary Dreaming

We dream
and wonder
what we mean.
Sometimes we know
and bow
in supplication.

Extraordinary Dreaming

After my amazing experience of being at one with the galaxy at the age of eleven, I didn't have another of that certain kind while awake.

When I was twenty, Bob was reclining with me beside him. He began to describe to me what he was experiencing. He, too, was wide awake. He said he was being guided and instructed by an ancient teacher. He repeated what he was hearing. It had to do with the planes of existence of the worlds. Bob said, "Sickness doesn't matter. That is not us. We are so much more than these bodies we occupy"

I was listening and confused by his being on two planes of consciousness at the same time. By his being somewhere else I couldn't sense, yet totally aware of my presence, talking to me as if this were ordinary.

Though I didn't have another experience, of that certain kind, while awake, there were four while I slept. These occurred over a period of more than two decades. Unlike typical dreams, these precognitive experiences were very different. They were vivid and never a doubt was there about their complete recall. They were given, like a gift, to be remembered, understood, and to help.

The first one was when I was about fifty. I had received the phone call the day before and immediately booked a flight to the East Coast. My niece was dead. It was a very cold winter on the East Coast. Bob stayed in California with a respiratory condition. It was our first time apart since we had remarried a few years before. I felt pulled between staying and going, but knew how much it would mean to my brother for me to go to his daughter's funeral.

I woke about 5:00 AM and didn't go back to sleep. I told Bob this dream that had awakened me, as he drove me to the airport:

I am on a plane. The flight attendant stopped next to me and asked, "Would you like chicken, chicken, or chicken?" I laughed and said, 'I'll have chicken.'"

When I was on the plane a few hours later, feeling emotional about Laurie's death, Lou's loss, and leaving Bob alone, the flight attendant pulled his cart up to me and apologized, "All we have left is chicken."

I had the certainty that I had made the right choice in going.

The next dream was also about 5:00 AM. We were visiting friends who had moved from the Bay Area to the Gold Country. I deferred to Bob's preference to stay at a nearby motel rather than with our friends.

My sleep was fitful. I looked forward to the event of the next day. Our plan was to buy a trip down a mountain hill where we would have a bar-b que dinner and pan for gold.

I woke with the words in my head, *"I can't jump the jump."* That was all. I hadn't seen anything. I said to Bob, "I don't understand what that meant." We both tried to make sense of it and couldn't.

The open bed truck we rode in, down the narrow, one-way bumpy dirt road, that evening, was filled with others, all of us hungry and looking forward to doing like the original '49 ers. We sat on built-in benches, facing each other. Suddenly the truck came to an abrupt stop. There didn't seem to be anyplace where it could go except forward or back. To our left was a sheer drop. To our right was mountain. In the confusion we waited, not knowing what was wrong.

Finally, the driver said, "The truck died. We're going to have to get a jump start. It will take awhile, but another truck is on the way."

There was no harm done, just a nervous delay, and we had an enjoyable evening.

The main significance of that one to me was the feeling I got because I realized I could tune in at times to the unknown, as needed and appreciated.

The next time wasn't until about fourteen years later. I shared all kinds of dreams with Bob. He often helped me make the connections of ordinary dreams, then adding, "You have weird dreams."

So, with this dream, which I thought was just an ordinary one, I told Bob:

You and I are on a bus. You get up to leave. I call out, "Don't leave without me," as I rush down the aisle to reach you. You get off the bus without me. I rush after you and can't find you. As I search for you I see a dry creek bed where stone faces are in relief. You start out walking on them, but I am not able to follow you."

A week later we were told that Bob was dying.

I feel that the first two dreams about the plane trip and the truck ride were to prepare me, in their simple way, for the shock of my life.

It was only in retrospect that I understood.

About a year after Bob died, I suggested to friends that we go to see a new Robin Williams film, *What Dreams May Come*. These friends sometimes suggested going to a movie with me. It was my first time to do that. I like Robin Williams and knew nothing about the film. He played the part of a widower who tries to follow his wife to the other side. At first he couldn't continue when he came to stone faces embedded in the ground.

In the film, being fiction, unlike my life, he did get beyond them.

I'll never know what Bob perceived when I had shared my dream with him, as I assiduously looked in my dream book for a clue. There was none.

The fourth dream happened a few years after Bob died. We had bought an old BMW that needed major mechanical work. Bob loved that car. I took care of it after he died and kept it going on its rebuilt engine and the dual carburetors our mechanic had slipped in, which he told us about after he had done a test-drive late one night on Highway 101 at 130-rniles an hour.

I had heard about getting a safety check done on cars before taking long trips. I went to the mechanic we had changed to, a German man who specialized in German cars.

I said, "I'll be driving to Sacramento and want you to check everything."

The next day Riki and I went to Concord where we stayed overnight at Jaki's apartment, before leaving for Sacramento to visit my grand-daughter Lori and her children.

At breakfast, in Concord, I shared this dream:

I am driving and there are obstacles in front of me that are like big buildings. I feel that as long as I stay calm, everything will be all right.

Driving to Sacramento felt like being on a race track. Everyone on the two lane road was driving 85-miles an hour. I was afraid if I slowed down we'd get hit from behind.

Coming back the next day on the same road, drivers were doing their usual, at least five miles an hour over the speed limit—but not going 85.

All of a sudden, I said, "I don't have any brakes!"

I never felt such a sense of responsibility for the safety of anyone else's life as I did then.

I asked each of my daughters to think of the best thing they could suggest. Jaki began praying. Riki said, "Use the hand brake." As I followed the building-like trucks in front of us, I said, "I'd better not. That might make us spin into them. I'm not getting off here until I see an exit that leads to a gas station."

Finally, after daring to stay on that truck trafficked road, going 65-miles an hour without brakes, I took an exit that said, "Gas."

I knew I'd have to use the hand brake then, not to run into the gas tanks, the building, or anyone standing there.

With a quick pull on the brake, we stopped. I asked the man watching our grand arrival to look under the hood and see what was wrong.

He said, "We only sell gas and some groceries."

It was almost 6:00 PM on a Friday night. He said, "A friend of mine works at a foreign car place just down the road. Tell him I sent you."

I had to drive across the exit road we had just survived.

They were still open. A quick look showed what the problem was, "It's the brake cylinder."

I said, "I just got the car checked over."

He said, "That can happen anytime to any car. I can get you a new part tomorrow. "

I had gotten long-distance towing insurance and could have been towed back to the Bay Area. I decided I'd rather get the car fixed and drive it back.

"Where's the closest, reasonable, non-seedy motel you can take us to?" I asked.

He said they just remodeled Motel 6 near where we were, outside of Davis.

Hungry, tired, we checked in and walked the few feet to a place called Cindy's next door. They had a dinner special, everything. We three all ordered that.

Then we gradually began to unwind and talked about what we had just been through. I felt shaky, grateful, and amazed at what dreams are made of.

DR. KATZOFF ON SAFETY OF KISSING

*I met him twice.
The first was through his friend
at the health food store.
I made an appointment
for I can't remember what.
I walked through his doorway
with a big silly grin
to see lengths of tape
he had hanging on the door frame
waiting for his patients' skin.
"That's very good," he enthused. "You are happy!"*

*I battled with myself whether to enjoy
my private amusement
or explain. Being young and naive
I began to explain.
But this doctor
of many decades, who had never married
and had written a book
on the subject of marriage, was off on his own
path of delight.
"I am glad to see you are so happy."
I thought if he reached
for one of those tapes I would burst into laughter.
He told me, "When I was in medical school
they taught us: always be sure to make your house calls
promptly, otherwise
the patient might recover before you arrive."
Together we laughed, he in his world, I in mine.*

*The next time we met was about three decades later.
He was quoted in a book called,*

"The Experts Speak—The Definitive Compendium of Authoritative Misinformation."
He was in a book of good company.
His quote: "A genuine kiss generates so much heat it destroys germs."
That may not be so—
but I think he destroyed them
with his innocent eccentricities.

Smidgen John

On Christmas Eve, Bob and I walked the short distance from our apartment building to our neighbors. The grounds were lush with many kinds of plants and trees. There was a manmade creek alongside the building they lived in. The curving sidewalk had a section made of wood. Beneath the wood was the creek, and somewhere there was the sound, "Ribet, ribet," from the frog we never saw. We could hear the frog as we approached the creek. When we reached the wood planking, the frog was silent. When we passed over the creek and were a few feet beyond, we heard, again, "Ribet, ribet."

I used my own apartment key to get into the building and when I rang our hosts' apartment bell, Louise called out, "Come in. The door is open."

I saw the tall, blonde girl I had spoken with once or twice. Louise introduced her older daughter. The girl seemed happy in a flighty sort of way. Her eyes didn't seem to focus. She seemed pleasant.

Marty, Louise's husband, typically quiet, apologized for being even quieter than usual. He said, "You know how some people get around the holidays. I get so depressed."

Louise said that John might be over in a while. I wondered, "Who's John?"

"Oh, he lives in the apartments," Louise said, moving between the dining area and kitchen as fast as her painful feet would allow.

The apartment was filled with the delicious smells of whatever she was cooking. "Excuse me," she said, "Help yourselves to cheese and crackers. I have to get back to the kitchen before the gravy burns."

Bob and I settled in with the happy daughter and the depressed husband, nibbling on the offered cheese and making conversation.

The doorbell rang. "Come in," sang Louise, "The door's open."

"Hi, I walked into the building with a couple who was just coming in."

Louise said," Glad you could make it. Your key would open the building door. They're all the same here."

After introducing John, Louise said, "Eat some cheese. I hope you can stay for dinner, too." That was the first time Bob and I knew that we were expected to stay for dinner.

John said, "Oh, I have to leave soon. I'm expected for dinner tonight with some other people. But it sure smells good in here."

John soon had Marty smiling. Louise got both their daughters to set the table. She had cooked a complete turkey dinner. Louise and both daughters were soon making trip after trip to the table with huge platters of steaming hot food.

John stopped in the middle of an anecdote, "Louise, your cooking smells so good, maybe I'll have just a smidgen." She smiled, "Good. I hope it came out good." John continued his anecdote. Marty visibly relaxed. Everyone began taking food. But John took very little, saying, "I have to be able to eat dinner later." He tasted the food and rolled his eyes upward. "This is the best food I've ever eaten in all my whole life." John was a small man, maybe twenty-nine or thirty years old. He was warming up to his small plate of food with a gourmet's indulgence. The younger daughter said, "My mom's a great cook."

Louise beamed, "John, you hardly took any. You can handle more than that." He wiped his mouth, as though he were going to save his appetite, "I'm going to a feast later." Everyone watched him to see what he would do next. "Maybe I'll have just a smidgen more." One by one, the heavy platters were passed to John, and his plate was soon heaped with food. He ate. Everyone ate with him as he extolled the genius of Louise's cooking. Marty felt more his usual quiet self. He had shed the feeling of responsibility to have a good time because it was a holiday season.

Louise told their daughters, "My feet have had it. Bring some more mashed potatoes and turkey." John said, "Not for me." The girls went dutifully into the kitchen with the platters and brought them out filled with more food.

John said, "Well, maybe just a smidgen, and then that's all."

Everyone was full and finished. John took the newly stocked platters which were passed to him, and proceeded to add turkey and mashed potatoes next to the vegetables and cranberry sauce on his plate.

When he finished, long after everyone else had finished, he offered to help clear the table. "Thanks, the girls will do it," Louise said.

The older daughter got up to show me the new long dress she had just bought. She was an attractive girl, statuesque, like a model. "I got it at this neat place in the city. It's from the twenties!"

While the girls cleared the table, Louise rested her aching feet and the men got more acquainted. Then John looked at his watch and said, "It's getting late. I have to be going to the feast."

I Know

Lucid waking
is more like a dream
than dreams are.
The entire world
is seen as
the reality of vibrating,
pulsing, unstoppable movement.
It is shocking and wonderful
in the same breath,
too much to bear
too long.

Joe's Story

We arrive at the Wilmington Airport, not having checked our flight schedule with the airline as I usually do.

After a fine farewell dinner with Lorrie and Joe, we learn that our first of three flights has flown.

It seems they notified me in October. I get that old guilt feeling and wonder if I printed that email and just glanced too quickly, not noticing the change. Or could it have been one they sent after that, when I could send, but not receive emails till I got help to right that problem.

We console ourselves with the truth: there is always a reason for everything. Maybe the reason, I'm still feeling guilt, is what I wrote above.

Karen calls Lorrie's cell phone, asking her to come back and get us. She calls Josh and tells him we'll be a day later. I call my housemate Jen and tell her, asking her to call off two appointments I had made.

Our schedule for the following day is what we will have to make the best of. After reaching Charlotte, North Carolina, then flying from there to Las Vegas, we have a nine hour layover in Vegas before the hour or so flight to Fresno.

Gambling bores me after a few minutes. We can't help wondering—neither of us gamblers—if this is all about a generous win at the slots via the twenty dollars max we're each willing to try.

It's a long time to wait for a short ride home.

Fortunately, Lorrie and Joe are good sports and back went our luggage into their van, for another night at their home.

They said, "We'll be able to take you to the Cracker Barrel for breakfast."

I'd never been to one, and all three looked forward to sharing the experience with me—the great breakfast and homey gift shop.

After ordering, we use the food prep time to look at the gift shop. When I come back to our table there are gifts for Karen and me at our placemats. Mine, because I'm such a purple lover is in that color: a fancy notebook, with fancier matching pen.

Lorrie and Joe tell me they want me to come back again, with or without Karen. I am touched.

On the way to the Cracker Barrel Joe asked me a question. During our week stay with them he, a retired forensic specialist, had asked me quite a few questions. It is his nature and his training. Now I see where Karen gets it from. I enjoyed answering his questions, always as curious as he, as to what my answers would come out like.

But this time I was resistant, as was Lorrie, when he asked, "Did you ever hear of the plane crash in San Diego?"

At the same time that I'm trying to recall, to answer Joe's question, I say, "This isn't a good time for plane crash conversation." Lorrie echos me.

Then Joe, as far as I'm concerned, unveils the reason for our flight fiasco.

He says, "I was going to be on that flight. My brother made me a birthday party in the Bay Area and I was supposed to be coming back home to San Diego on it. I don't remember why I took a later plane. When we landed, the plane staff were all pointing, and from the looks on their faces, I knew something had happened."

I asked what year that was. Lorrie remembered, "I had just moved to San Diego. I saw the smoke from the crash. Two planes, a small and larger one, had collided. It was in 1979."

Karen said, "I was eleven years old. You never told me!"

Joe said, "I called Jan, my wife, and told her I was all right. She had thought I was dead. So did all my co-workers. There were no survivors."

I was amazed to realize how much and how many lives would have been affected if Joe had taken his original flight.

Karen would not have had her dad. Lorrie and Joe would never have met.

We would never have been in the van now, on our way to the airport for our second try.

I asked Joe what feelings the experience brought out of him. In his quiet, unassuming way he said, "I was too busy dealing with my work."

"How long is it since you've talked about this to anyone after that?" I asked. "This is the first time," he said.

Ruth, Then and Now

When I look back
in memory
or even actuality
at pictures of my child years
I see only from the bridge
of my nose to the top of
some curly brown hair.
The rest is hidden
behind a captive cat,
like the big fluff of a muff
I saw in one photo
where I seemed surrounded in a coat to match.
All photos after that
hid me well
behind a large fluffy cat
in my little arms
covering front view
from bridge of nose
down to as far as cat
with tail could stretch.

It's well I saw myself like that
because I seem to have
no conscious memory
of what I valued then.

But now, with life experiences
to fill a treasure chest
I can see that little child
bundled in furry hat as well,

*and compare the me of then
with this one now.*

*I hope, worthy of comparison,
is what I see: From a child
I wouldn't recognize
I see joy in the moment,
caring for creatures
and unconditionality.*

*If that is still so
and I know when it comes to cats
I never grew up
then I think there's yet hope for me.*

The Waiting Room

She looked like angels look, if we could see them. It was really more a sensing of the feelings she radiated. Her cocoa brown face had a natural smile which was often there around her full lips like the whimsy of Dizzy Gillespie. It seemed to be always in her eyes. She sat several feet in front of me, facing the emergency room, a magazine on her rotund lap, her son, wearing a bright baseball cap, to her left.

The little girl with her was constantly moving. She went to the low desk-like counter in front of the office and lighted for a moment, like a butterfly. Her momma said, with interest, "What are you doing over there?"

The girl looked happy, "I'm ordering hamburgers and French fries." She put the imaginary food into her mouth, "Ummmmmm."

I was sitting, reading about a young girl in a short story. The one in front of me held my attention more. It wasn't what she said or did, at that point, because eating as she was, is universal with children. I was attracted to the good feelings that went directly to her, like one often sees with niece and aunt, or grandchild and grandparent. This relationship was a comfortable one, as easygoing interplay of souls related. The boy looked up at me from his magazine and made some pleasant comment. He had a smile, too, that went straight to the heart. I didn't hear what he said. But I felt it.

The little girl went to the water fountain and turned it on. While she managed to coordinate a drink with the pushing of a button, her mother asked, "Can you get it?" The girl, by way of explanation and answer to such a question, stated, "I'm four." She took another mouthful of water and her brother got up to get some, too. The girl came and sat beside me. A large drop of water flew off from her onto my bare arm. I ignored the water and smiled. I laughed, enjoying this little imp and a mother who could enjoy her, too.

The girl went to another corner of the room behind her mother. Her mother turned and firmly said, "Swallow that water." She swallowed it.

The girl came back and flounced onto the seat beside me, which was attached to mine. The chairs made a small scraping sound. The girl said, "Ouch." I said, "Ouch, said the chair." She didn't believe she heard that. "What?"

"Ouch, said the chair," I repeated.

Once again she asked, and once again I repeated it.

She moved around the room again, now climbing on a chair directly behind her mother. Her mother said, "You're always moving, aren't you!"

She came and plunked onto the chair beside me again. She smiled, "Ouch, said the chair."

I said, "Oh, you liked that."

She asked, "What are you reading about?"

"About a little girl."

"How old is she?"

"About ten."

She added sagely, "Maybe she's eleven."

Then, while she began to touch my hair, she said, "My brother's ten."

She asked me to read her the sign on the wall. I read her part of it, told her about some of it. She was getting fancy with my hair by now. I liked the way her mother allowed us this friendship and didn't interfere by telling her to leave the lady alone.

The girl's touch was gentle with my hair. She began to twist the side section around itself.

"I'm making a braid," she told me.
I said, "You're twisting it. This is what a braid is like." I parted the same section of hair in three and alternated it into a braid.

"Are you making it tight?" she asked.

I let her look and feel it. "Do you have braids?" I found one of her tiny, tight little braids with my fingers.

Her mother said, "She loves to play with hair."

"I braid my momma's hair," the girl said proudly.

I said, to the mother, "That's good. Maybe she'll be a beautician."

Her mother said, "She calls it beauty-tician. "

The four of us had a laugh with that one, as the girl tried recalling how she usually says it.

Her mother smiled, "She twists the hair and calls that braiding." She asked me if I thought they were very busy tonight, indicating the emergency room. I didn't know, either, and asked how long she'd been waiting. She looked up at the clock, "Since about eight fifteen." It had been a half hour. Her boy had a yellow hospital wrist band on, and there was no one in the room besides us.

The little girl continued making twist braids in my hair. Her small chocolate brown hand touched my arm.

"Why are your hands so cold?" I asked.

Matter-of-factly, she said, "Because I was outside."

The girl said, "Why are you here?"

"It's a secret."

We giggled.

She said, "'Cause you're waiting for the doctor."

A nurse came to the doorway. The three got up and followed her. Both children were quite tall. The woman's size, till then, somewhat hidden because she was sitting, was enormous. Her body was as big as her inner beauty. She wore a printed, faded, cotton dress. It reminded me of that old song Sinatra used to sing, "She may get weary. Women do get weary, wearing the same shabby dress. But, when she's weary, try a little tenderness."

"Tenderness" could have been her middle name.

I ran my fingers through my hair to remove the twist braid and continued waiting.

Waiting for a Friend to Pick Up her Prescription

A woman sitting left of me
tells me I have beautiful hair,
the way it waves
the way it falls,
she motions with her hands.
I thank her
saying it is getting to
a beautiful white
like hers.
Then she speaks softly
motioning to the walls
around us.
I miss her words.
When I say I couldn't hear
she doesn't seem to hear.
I repeat, pointing to my ear,
And then again, as she continues,
no use, I see.
I could sit next to her
instead of the empty chair
between us.
But I don't know what illness
brings her here.
A man comes to her,
"Time to go," he says.
She knows him
I can see,
but doesn't quite agree.
Patiently, gently, he urges once again.
As she stands he tells me simply,
"Dementia."

"I thought maybe"...I say.
"She's ninety. What can we expect,"
he says, his attitude one of caring.

Now outside, we walk past them.
He had placed a little platform
beside the open door of his truck
and was helping her to
take the step to enter.
His expression, as he glanced
one last time at me,
said, "She is my mother.
I will always love and protect her
no matter what it takes."

With Hands Out

I carried my white jacket. It was too warm to wear it. I had finished work and had gone to the bus stop, feeling tired from the unusual muggy weather.

A black woman, who must have weighed two hundred forty pounds, was standing there, and seemed to be waiting for a bus. She said, "Do you work here?" referring to the hospital behind us.

"Yes."

"Where do you work?"

"In an office." I glanced over her shoulder to see if a bus were coming.

"Do you work for a doctor?"

"No. There are a lot of office jobs that have nothing to do with doctors."

The woman boldly asked another question, "Are you Italian?"

I had often been taken for Italian or Spanish, sometimes French. People seemed curious about me, so I accepted it.

"No, I'm not Italian."

"What _are_ you?"

I told her the answer to her question, feeling like this lady was more than simply curious, but I wasn't able to put my finger on it. It was a personal, harmless question, that I didn't ask of others because what did it matter. But this woman persistently queried me in a way that made me look for my bus when I sensed it wasn't yet visible.

I said, in jest, "Are you Italian?"

The woman didn't respond to my facetiousness, but instead asked another question, "Do you know anyone who can use a housekeeper?"

Before I could respond, the woman said, "I can't get any work because since the Vietnam War the only ones who get anything are those damned Vietnamese and the Mexicans."

I listened to her go on and on, criticizing and complaining. I felt like walking away from this woman, but knew a few steps away would not be far enough. The bus was a few minutes late and would whisk me away like a magic carpet any moment.

"Come closer," the woman said. The only teeth in her mouth that I could see were two long ones in the upper front, and four on the bottom, two at either side. I stood still.

The woman said, "Why are you afraid of me?"
"I can hear you from here. Because I don't want to come closer doesn't mean I'm afraid of you."

The woman said she couldn't find any work and again cursed the other cultures because they got aid and she couldn't.

"Have you gone to the welfare office?"
"Yeah," she snarled, "They won't help me. They kicked me out."

I didn't even want to look at my watch or down the street for the bus again. It hadn't been this late since the bus strike ended. My experiences hadn't prepared me for someone like this. I felt trapped.

"I don't have a place to stay. I live on the street."
"Couldn't you put an ad up in a market and give a friend's phone number?"

"I was staying with these rich Iranians, but..."

This lady has an answer and a rebuttal for everything, I thought. Stop trying so hard with her.

The big woman took a quick, stealthy step and she was beside me.

"You know, people say fat people don't get hungry. But that's not true. I'm hungry. You have no idea how good one of those juicy hamburgers on a bun with lettuce and tomatoes tastes. Will you give me the money to get one?"

My compassionate side had no conflict with my quick answer. I looked into the dark glasses and said firmly, "No."

The woman took off her glasses then, as a challenge, and looking at me, directly in my eyes, asked, "Why not?"

"I don't choose to."

"Don't you believe in helping people?"

We waited, perfectly still, eyeing each other. I had nothing left to say. I didn't see a person down on her luck, but a rapier sharp con artist who could have been highly successful had she gone into door to door sales.

As in years gone by, I felt the strength of those who know their own weakness, and did not give in to my own naivete.

If my friend, Anita, had not come by, just then, I wondered what the woman would have tried next. Anita walked to the bench and sat beside me. We began talking in the free and easy way we had between us. The big woman hung around. Then, standing in the doorway, filling it with her girth, she interrupted, "You never answered my question." I waited. Which question, I wondered. "Do you know anyone who needs a housekeeper?"

"No, I don't."

"That's really something. I talk to a thousand women who all go to work, and nobody knows of anyone."

I thought of the shy lady who comes to my apartment to clean, and lets herself in each time with the extra key I'd had made for her. I winced, mentally, to think of what I would come home to if this one had the key.

Seeing Anita and me ignoring her, the woman walked a few feet away to where a woman was parking in front of the hospital.

I told Anita about my experience with the woman. We both watched as the aggressive woman stood in the street talking to the lady who had parked.

I said, "I never met anyone like her. The only time I ever saw people begging was years ago in San Francisco. They stayed in one spot and if anyone wanted to put money in their hat or their hand, they could."

Anita and I kept watching the woman who had been hounding me. She listened to the conversation between her and the woman who had just parked and was fishing in her purse for parking change. Anita said, "I'm going to go see if that woman wants any help."

I felt touched by her humanism. The fact that Anita was seventy and half the size of the agitator had never entered her mind. She left her belongings on the bench beside me and went to the woman. They came back together and the woman went on her way. The big one finally left.

The bus arrived. We rode with the incident for a while, still on our minds. Anita said, "I just couldn't see her bothering that woman."

Anita and I had a budding friendship. It began at the bus stop, and, over a period of months, we met occasionally. Anita worked part time. She was a sensitive person. She'd lived in a large family where the door was always open to strays: people or pets. She'd had to take responsibility for herself at a young age. It was apparent that self-sufficiency was second nature to her.

No Pollyanna, but when the bus arrived, Anita's face lit up, "Good. He's on time and we get to have the nicest driver."

We only rode together for about three miles. My stop always seemed to be too soon when we did.

Because the moments before had been as they had, Anita said, "My husband was a double amputee. One day I was walking down the street and a man, with one leg, was on the street selling pencils. I gave him a dollar and then I began laughing so hard I couldn't stop. The man said, 'What is it, lady?' but I was laughing so hard I couldn't talk. My son, who was with me, asked me, too, why I was laughing. I finally was able to stop laughing and tell him. Then he couldn't stop laughing. Here I was giving a dollar to a man who had only one leg and I had a husband at home who had none."

IN COURT SCHOOL
Dedicated to the students in court school

*These dark, bleak halls
hide the hope and help
I see within the class,
a class of bright and loving ones
who only missed a beat or two
in the cacophony of their
young lives.
Here they learn more than
the required academics.
They find the meaning of trust
each one is born to.
They find each moment is a choice
in spite of pasts that they
endured.
They find that love is why we are.*

In the Midst of Plenty

We walked past the many booths of food, brilliant glazed ceramics, artwork of every kind, bright colorful clothing and live music every few feet. When we heard jazz we looked for seats. A friend was there. After warm greetings he brought three chairs together so we could listen in comfort.

The weather was just what people want for an outdoor arts and crafts festival, hot, but not too hot. There wasn't a strong breeze, just enough to keep from feeling too warm.

We spoke, catching up with ourselves since we'd last met. But mostly we listened to the good music we'd come to hear. His cousin plays piano. He's had a long-standing gig in San Francisco. There was a man on acoustic bass who'd had the same city gig with him for many years. The club owner dropped his costs and let him go. Just like the affluent town this festival was in: the same bass player —a fine musician—but that has nothing to do with it, was hired for part of the day. The cousin would have to solo the rest of the afternoon.

The bass player packed up and left. The piano player took a break. He stood, talking with someone, in front of the heavy wood lattice backdrop. The street, blocked off, had a green plastic covering where the musicians had set up.

Before anyone could react the tall weighty backdrop toppled, barely missing the piano player.

For a moment everything stopped in that little corner of the street fair. Nobody moved. Then people went back to their eating and conversation as though nothing had happened.

Colors swirled in the light breeze: multi-colored table umbrellas, rainbows of clothing, plates of ethnic Picasso-like varieties and colorful speech seemed to blend in the bright afternoon.

Out of a corner of the eye appeared a *nebech*. A *nebech* is a being for whom others feel anything from pity to contempt. He wore a wide brimmed dirty hat. His beard was long and thick and needed to be washed like all the rest of him. His huge winter coat had a zigzag tear big enough for him to put both feet through together. He looked like he had stepped out of a black and white movie into a technicolor world.

Without a word he reached to help the piano player lift the fallen backdrop. They set it on its side where it could do no damage.

That done, he walked back to the grocery cart that held his few possessions and left the festive scene.

One More Story

There is time for lunch
between job sites
at a park setting
where seniors eat
and socialize.
I barely have time
for eating.
But I stop there
anyway.
A way is made
for me to sit
even though
serving has begun.
A man who served with Patton
shares stories of the general—
his kindness and bravery
his amusing ways.
"People see him as something
else, but my experiences
were good," he says.
I never saw the movie.
Now I want to.
I apologize, saying, "I wish
I could stay, but
I have to get back to work."
I stand to leave
and he looks into my eyes,
"There's one more story
I want to tell you.
It's true."
As I stand he shares

his tale of
almost fifty years.
While in a war zone
he had to urinate.
"I walked over to some bushes," he said.
"Then I felt a hand on my shoulder
and heard a voice say, 'Jeff, move.'
Right after I moved away
a land mine exploded where I had been.
This is a true story," he repeated.
"Somebody up there was watching over me."

Freedom

I don't know why I remember the days I laid on my back on the backyard lawn with my brother, looking at cirrus clouds and describing the animals and silly shapes we saw. You'd think someone had offered me the whole weird world, it made me feel more good inside and out than I usually knew what the hell it was like to be.

I wish I'd remembered because three decades went by like a bullet train in Spain, which—years after—I lived to ride. But I almost forgot the ecstatic feelings that clouds allowed to seep into my being.

I was on my back on a huge front lawn imploring the feeling to return as I squinted into a fire sky, cloudless as an oven. This was my communal home where I could live any way I could imagine. I was existing in a kind of refuge, free of prison, free of an insane asylum. Only not free of myself.

I saw others come through who found us. Some, who behaved just like me, that I saw clear as rose water, were out of their minds.

Others at the commune warned me to watch out for one particular person.

I didn't think she had noticed me. I'd see her out in front, looking as lost as I felt. To me her dour, dumpy look hid the fact that she was dangerous.

I often wore a white floppy hat. I loved the way it brought me memories of a life I never knew.

One afternoon I finally decided to get busy and do something. I got out the iron, the board, my wrinkled clothes, set the iron to the hottest temperature, and pushed myself into action.

She came into the room so slowly, so quietly, she took my breath away.

Hello, I said, scared of her like I'd never been scared of anyone else before.

She didn't answer. Cat-quick she got behind me. Strong as a couple of healthy oxen, she grabbed my right arm that held the searing iron, at the same time her left pinned mine behind me.

You and your fancy hat, she jeered, holding the hot iron skin-close to my face, ready to brand me.

Her anger and insanity fueled her strength. I knew from somewhere deep inside that I didn't dare to struggle.

Gimme that hat. I want your hat. She held me like a vise.

You can have the hat.

Go get it right now.

On legs of melted ice I managed to get down the long hallway to get the hat, her soul-sick eyes never leaving me.

I was free, free of a life of disfigurement, free of her attack, free to remember to look at clouds.

In the Garden of Life

Stay in the garden of Life
where your own thoughts
embrace you
with the light
of your own making.

Stay and listen to the quiet
of your own being.
Still yourself
to hear the color
of your blossoms
that are the music
of your life.

Some of the Sounds of the Universe

We sat listening to chamber music. There were five instruments: flute, oboe, clarinet, French horn and bassoon.

The soothing, pleasant feelings they evoked reminded me of other sounds and other times. One of the earliest times, I don't even remember, but it's no less a part of me, because it happened. When I was a baby, my brother, George, used to practice violin each evening. Listening, I would fall into a peaceful sleep.

George put the violin aside, forever, but his feeling for classical music stayed with him. When I was a teenager, I used to work in our father's shop sometimes, after school, and on Saturdays. George would be standing beside a pot of molten metal, pouring it from a long handled ladle into a mold, all day. He had the radio behind him on a station from which music soared beyond the steaming heat, which separated us, and out the always opened windows in back of him. I knew stirrings of emotions, provoked by sounds, that I hadn't known I had. Some sounds made me sad; others made me feel like I was soaring right out the window, too.

Someone told me that when he moved to the mid west, a new friend told him that one could hear the corn growing. The newcomer thought he was being kidded, but at the other's insistence, they went out one day, to the arid garden, and heard the sound of corn pushing its way up out of the ground. He was surprised to not only hear it grow, but to see it, as well.

I must have seen almost a thousand movies as a child before I was conscious of the moods designed by background music to create effects.

When my friend decided to finally see "ET," she bought the sheet music and played it before going to the theatre. When I visit her and she sits at her piano to play, she seems to be in a state of total delight.

Once I saw a film in the Mill Valley Library about the sounds of water. It was a short film with only the sounds that moving water makes, when it's running or dripping, a film of waterfalls and waves that break near shore. For once I enjoyed the staccato of a dripping faucet. It was a concert unto itself.

When I first moved to Mill Valley, I thought I'd never sleep past daybreak again. Across the street, every early morning, a rooster broke the dawn. After a few mornings, I slept right through it.

When I met Eve and her husband, she told me, as she drove her car that the only sound she could hear was a siren. Their children both learned to read when they were two years old because Eve and her husband were deaf. She smiled and said, "My children are my ears."

One of the most soothing sounds in nature, I think, is the rain, when it falls softly. I like the sounds of water dripping from the eves.

I loved the sounds of my husband's bass fiddle. He made his own music. And that is what matters to me.

My Brain

I hardly dare to take a look
the left is so determined.
It writes for me
designs my room
creates a purple haven.
It satisfies my every whim,
assures me I'm behavin'.
It's constantly my prime companion
no matter where I am
and rests me assured
that I Am, I Am, I Am.

I hardly know just where to look
my right is kind of hiding.
It double books,
and malaprops
and keeps slip and sliding.
It cons my choices
makes me aware
of omelets on my face.
It's constantly my prime suspect
no matter where I am
and rests me assured
I'm not inured
that I only think I am.

I Don't Know Why,
But I Always Wanted to See Livermore

I don't know if it's just the name that got to me or because that nice couple we met moved there or what. Maybe the fact that a couple of years before we had gotten into the car one day to look around the surrounding area and came within the outskirts of the town before we decided it was too hot, and turned around without seeing Livermore. I don't know why I wanted to visit Livermore. Maybe, by some perversity, because the name reminded me of an illness I had once incurred in Mexico.

We were on our way back, down 205, from the Mother Lode, on the way home from a few days trip. All had gone as planned. The motel room we'd reserved in Jackson the month before was, as promised, overlooking a creek with a small waterfall. There were ducks, and geese, as we had been told. The sheep, just beyond them, walked in slow, regal high stepping motion, like the prizewinning animals they were, the ewes close behind. We sat on our patio and relaxed into the tempo of Jackson. We laughed when the sheep's pace turned to running, as someone approached the fence in the distance, with a hand full of food.

It was the naturalness of the environment that made the place so special. We fed the ducks the "home made" rolls we'd saved from lunch. It was the goose who didn't want to go into the water, who stood on the narrow stone ridge, between levels of cascading water, stretching an already long neck to eat the, by then, water soaked piece of roll. The goose wagged his tail feathers like a puppy. It was the goose who panted just like a dog before and after each morsel, that amused us in the setting sun.

Someone named Maud had answered when I had phoned to make our reservations. When I'd asked, "Is there such a thing as a room with a view?" she'd answered, "I'm glad you asked. I'll give you one." That's when I learned of the creek and the animals. In my excitement I had forgotten to ask the price and she hadn't mentioned it. With the ambience and the continental breakfast included, it cost us a little more than one third the rate of a three diamond city hotel.

Maud, with her hair drying in curlers, came by with a 1926 calendar for us. "Save it for 1982. It's the same." We felt almost as though we lived in the era of the cars that were in profile on each page. And, with the best of both worlds, we recruited Maud to take our picture, which we three admired less than a minute later.

The next day we walked up and down steps that were part of the sidewalk in Sutter Creek. Somehow the weather was not too hot or too cold. We saw as much and as little of everything we had set out to see. Without feeling rushed we moved along as planned. The next overnight stay was, once again, as we had prearranged. We had even, somehow, coordinated our appetites with the old fashioned ice cream parlor recommended by our friendly auto mechanic supervisor. The eighty year old secret recipe for their ice cream was well kept and worth the wait.

In Auburn we found more sidewalk stairs and walked to pose beside the statue of a kneeling gold miner panning for gold. Its size was like that of King Kong's to Fay Wray. I could have fit the pan to overflowing, and had I been made of gold, that miner would never have had to stoop again. But he was made of stone, and I—as the saying goes—was only "good as gold."

With our few precious photos, maps and mementos we started our trip home to the Bay Area. Our complimentary menu, from the ice cream parlor recommended by our auto mechanic, was among our collection. We had seen him the day before we left, as we assured ourselves that our '73 car was fit for the trip.

We were about twelve miles out of Tracy, thinking of stopping at Livermore for a stretch and refreshment when the old '73 motor stopped dead. Bob made a quick turn out of the right lane onto the generous emergency roadside strip. He looked under the hood and we both wished, then, that we knew a lot about cars. Everything looked fine. The new battery looked good. Nothing was unattached. Bob stood by the car, waving his arms for someone to stop. It could have taken a long time of waving before someone stopped. We knew that. And so did the man who stopped less than a minute later. He was in his late twenties, or early thirties. He said, "Not many people will stop nowadays." When Bob offered him change to phone the auto club, the man said, "I've got change. I just hope someone will stop for me someday."

Sunsets, our daily treasure, so often go unnoticed, by me, by many others. I watched the sun over the hills of Livermore. It was as though I watched thousands of slides, each one different, during that hour. The sky was a changing watercolor of hues. I felt a detachment as we sat and waited that was aided by the constantly changing view out the dusty car window. We talked, mostly about the car and what we might expect to happen. I didn't want to get upset about our situation. Stuck as we were, I didn't feel worried or anxious, being with my husband. My calm was contagious. Just as the sun was fading from view the tow truck arrived. I only regretted that we didn't know the name of the man who had phoned them for us.

We sat in the cab of the truck while our car followed in tow. In a few minutes the sky was in darkness. Ed, the driver, said he would take us to a station in town where he knew them. "If they can't fix it, I'll take you to another guy's place I know. He's closed now, but he told me he'll be there tomorrow." It was Friday of the Memorial Day Weekend. Jim offered to give us a ride to a hotel if the first station couldn't fix the problem. We were both touched by his humanity. It's true not many people would stop to help like the driver had who called the auto club. It's also rare for someone on a job to extend himself as much as Ed was offering to for us. Right after I thought of the idea and the amount, Bob said, "I'm going to give him five dollars." I told him, "That's exactly what I just thought of doing." Ed was a serious looking guy, and when Bob slid the five dollar bill into his breast pocket he smiled kind of shyly, and, appreciatively he said, "All right!"

They tried their best under the hood and the car wouldn't start. Calls kept coming in to Ed from the dispatcher. He asked us if it would be OK with us if he responded to another call first. We were grateful for a ride to a hotel. The first call he responded to was nowhere around. Ed called the dispatcher back and repeated the location where he was waiting, so then the dispatcher got it straight.

Ed had been told the car needed a jump start. The three of us arrived with our car in back. The man with car trouble said, "I had a jump start and it didn't work. I need to be towed."

Ed asked him if he'd mind if he dropped our car off first and took us to a hotel. He was patient and we thanked him.

We left our car off and Jim got a call to open a car door. A woman had locked her keys inside. We arrived and saw her waiting by the car in front of a market with a bag of groceries.

By now we'd been getting to know Ed for almost two hours. He was an action oriented person, wiry and strong. Bob asked him, "Have you played a lot of sports? You seem athletic." Ed answered, "Yes, I've played basketball and baseball, and just about everything else; you name it."

We were getting tired just watching him jump from the high cab, hoisting and attaching. After he hooked up the van we had come back to, he said, "I need to get gas. I don't want to run out of gas." I looked at the dashboard. It showed empty. I agreed, "We don't want to be stuck twice tonight." We pulled into a gas station, our luggage out in back, the towed van attached, with the man who'd had the jump start that didn't work, following us with his wife in her car.

Ed apologized several times during the evening for delaying our arrival at a hotel. There was a clean and less expensive motel next to the station. If they had no vacancy he would take us to the fancier one by the highway. Bob went to check. No vacancy. He phoned the other one. They had lots of vacancies. Ed had mentioned he hadn't had a chance to eat dinner. It was nearing ten thirty and he said, "I probably won't get any sleep tonight." He'd been working since eight that morning. The dispatcher called him with new distress calls. Ed went to the two machines at the front of the station and came back with a can of soda and a couple of big chocolate chip cookies. He took a gulp of the soda, set it between his legs, and held one of the cookies in his mouth while he drove out of the self serve station. I asked, "Is that dinner?" He said, "Right now I'll take anything I can get." Then in a few bites he added, "I've got a good pot of chili waiting for me at home." Curious, I asked, "Who does the cooking at your house?" He laughed, "I do!" and together we agreed, "That's why it's good."

Till now Ed had been businesslike, friendly, but not a big talker. Now we were towing the other vehicle where the driver wanted to go home, and Bob mentioned how impressed we were with Ed's endurance. "Yeah, I'm healthy. I'd have to be to do this." Bob said, "My wife mentioned that not only were you an action person, but that you use your head, too." Ed told us he had gone to college for four years, taking industrial design. We said his job was tough work and we were tired just from watching him. As we neared an intersection, which by now was familiar, he said, "I used to drive a delivery truck by the Embarcadero. After that this is easy. Then I used to work for a company repossessing cars. I had to repossess bikes from Hell's Angels." He told us that it was between two and six in the morning when he worked then. He got the job done without confrontations that way. He warmed to his subject when he recalled the times he repossessed police cars which were parked illegally. "The police didn't like me very well. They'd put me in jail and then I got bailed out. But they had to pay their fine and extra waiting time for my delay."

We had left off the other people and were on our way to the hotel. Ed said, "Here's my card. If you can't get the car fixed tomorrow call me if you need help."

We took the steep step down from the truck cab and checked in to the hotel, worn and getting hungry again. No, the dining room closed at ten PM. It was ten forty. There was no food available till six the next morning.

On our vacation I had doggy bagged like I would when eating out near home. There's always more than I can eat. We had kidded about whether ducks like eggplant parmesan and had almost forgotten we had it. We checked it out and it was still good. We needed it then more than the ducks would have before.

The next morning we took a cab to our car. Cab service in town had begun three weeks before, we were told. We saw less of Livermore by daylight than we had the evening before. The garage owner got on the phone after he looked under the hood. "Come back in an hour and a half, it'll be ready." It turned out we needed a new fuel pump and points. We walked to the nearest food place that was open, a deli about a block and a half away. As we were finishing our lunch, Jo, the owner, came toward us with a piece of baklava on a napkin. "Do you like sweets?" she asked. "You should never have asked," I grinned. She said, "This piece got cut off too short and I thought you might like to share it." We began talking. She told us about her first experience away from home—getting the bus back to Nebraska when she was seventeen. A warm, gregarious lady, she sat at our table, talking about her appreciation of meeting different types of people. It was the regional differences she found so interesting. Her teenaged assistant was ready for a break, Jo told her, "Help yourself to something to eat." The thin girl busied herself getting what she wanted, then came and sat at the table next to ours. We continued talking and Jo looked over at the teenager who was having iced tea and two exotic looking pastries," Is that all you're going to have?" The girl looked content, "Yes." Jo continued, "That's why I like to travel."

Bob told her, "My wife likes to travel, too."

I said, "People are mostly what it's all about." We told them about our unexpected stay in Livermore. "I always wanted to see Livermore," I said.

Equinox

*Looking at my own mortality
I don't want to hasten passage
through the stages of immortality.*

*This mortal life
has served me well
in spite of myself.*

*Now I have reached
the turning point
where balance insists
to be chosen,
a small price
for a great chapter
in the unfathomable.*

The Thrift Shop

Beyond religion, beyond any sect at all, the feeling in this area was sacred for the preservation of quiet, contemplative thought. Or no thought.

It was not the ordinary run of thrift shops. This one was cloistered from the world. It was approached beneath an arched way from one direction. And from the other path there was a garden with stone seats among tall trees.

Each time I walked into the atmosphere of this ancient churchyard, I felt a weightlessness of serenity, as if I had actually stepped out of my body into a higher plane.

On three sides the church was edged with streets of traffic, the smells and noise of cars and buses. But the trees absorbed sound, the green lawns cushioned away distractions.

I stepped beneath the sign that simply said, Thrift Shop, and walked the one flight down.

I've asked myself, "If money were no object?" would I still indulge this hobby. I think I would. It is like the mountain to a climber, or a treasure hunt. It is the fun of the find. A place that sometimes raises the question, "I like it. What is it?"

I had no doubt this time. What I found had its designer label clearly identifying the jeans and matching top.

I wandered about, holding my find and looking at things while a very short volunteer walked behind me, watching me with a practiced eye.

I walked back to the only dressing room and a lady stepped into it just as I approached. One of the volunteers offered the use of the room beyond the shuttered doors. I went there and tried on the jeans. The one who had been watching me came in and sat down. We discussed the fit. I could move the button. I hadn't thought of that.

She said, "We're not supposed to let people go back here. Some of them change the price tags and some steal."

I thanked her for trusting me.

She said, "I'm the manager here. My husband died at the hospital next door twenty years ago. It was on Christmas Day and that was his birthday, too."

I listened, looking into her bright eyes.

"They didn't have volunteers there then. The next year before Christmas I went to that hospital and told them, "I want to work on Christmas Day." She smiled, "They couldn't get over that." As Christmas came closer I didn't get depressed like I could have. When I woke up on Christmas morning I felt I had a responsibility and I looked forward to the day. The first patient I visited looked up when she saw me and said, "Here comes Mary Sunshine!" I felt the chills of emotion as she shared her life with me.

She went on talking about the fact that she gave up the volunteering there because her work at the Thrift Shop turned into a full time job. She obviously enjoyed it, explaining their record keeping system for annual tax deductions.

I noticed a piece of cake on an opened, crinkled piece of foil, "That looks good."

"One of the volunteers baked it. Would you like to have it?"

"Thank you. I'll just taste it." As I reached to break off a sample she answered my next question, "It's carrot cake." A favorite of mine.

The woman spoke with appreciation for the volunteers who worked with her. "They're all good workers."

We agreed it was too bad there were people who would take things from the shop.

Then she looked back in her mind's eye to when she had married. She said, "I was so happy to live in San Francisco then. It's changed. There is so much crime now."

"It's sad," I said, "But we feel, my husband and I, that if everything were wonderful, we would be too attached to the world, and not want to leave for higher planes."

Then she, ever so slightly, put her face to the side, and said, "That's right. I never really thought about it that way. That's a good way to look at it."

The Marvelousness

*What does a poet do
when words are hardly adequate?
I watch and marvel
at the marvelousness
a feast for vision
but more than vision
can begin to see.
It is the realization
of all reality.
It is as though
nothing else can matter
but to simply be,
as pure, gentle snow
graces the world around me.*

What We Liked Best

When I think of the various jobs I have had, there is one outstanding. It was much more than a job to me. It was the fulfillment of a lifetime dream. And therefore I knew the feeling of incredulity to be getting paid for doing what meant so much to me.

I had been doing a job that felt oppressive, and decided I must do what I want, when I saw the ad in the local paper. They were looking for a housemother for six "young ladies" who varied in age from nineteen to thirtyone. After a long and thorough search they selected me.

The demands in energy, patience, emotion and understanding were high. When I first responded to their ad, I told them I hadn't finished college. I thought that would be a block in being considered, and wanted to find out before we went any further. The answer I received gave me hope, "We don't care." They wanted someone who did care and didn't feel college would give that to anyone. They also didn't want someone with preconceived ideas from something they had read in a book.

The early months were a trial for each of us, as, one by one, the women moved in and we began to know each other.

I worked in close conjunction with a county social worker. That's how I learned that one of the women in recent years past, in fits of temper, had broken over thirty pair of her prescription eyeglasses. She never did it after she moved in.

They each had their work, volunteer or school commitments. So weekends were their days of relaxation. I shared more than a hundred different places with them, from fairs and shopping, to concerts and movies, from walks on the beach, to a private van Gogh showing.

Before I met them, I met a woman who befriended me. She was my gracious hostess at her many acred ranch, and where she also loved hosting friends at her palatial home in town. I told her about my hopes for the job of housemother. When the job came through, she invited the seven of us to visit her at the ranch.

I remembered the feeling I'd had the first time I'd been there. It was deep in the country, trees so abundant and lush that that was all you could see, except for mountains in the distance. After getting out of the car I walked the narrow dirt path to a small opening in the greenery. There in the quiet walked peacocks proudly. A horse grazed in the distance. The long, low ranch house, built in the Mexican style, was like a warm greeting.

Driving home after dinner and picnicking, swimming and just enjoying, all six people told me, "Of all the places you took us to, guess where we liked it best!"

THURSDAY IS THANKSGIVING
A MOTHER'S VOICE

I want to place my arms about her.
I want to speak into her eyes with mine.
I listen to her read the book she chose from many
and tape her reading to her child.

It's just one Thursday till Thanksgiving
and she gives me thanks for being there.

I am free.
She is not.

To be there I was investigated and informed
not to wear anything metallic or denim.
Denim is the cloth
of those incarcerated there.

She reads with love,
knowing her voice will reach her child
as will the book she read,
her message on the tape and written in the book.

I am asked by my peers how it was for me.
One can't ignore the great rolls of barbed wire
on top of lofty fencing,
and knowing in a tower
even higher are guards with arms always ready.

How was it for me?
I want to place my arms about her.
I want to speak into her eyes with mine.
My one regret is that there was no time
for another.
Time is all they have
and I'll return with mine.

Revealment

Jeannie sat at the computer like she was creating at an organ. It was as big, and overlooked the entire small medical claims office. Her smiling face was the warmest part of the cold office. Cold office. In temperature and in vibration. My desk was at the front door. Each time a doctor or vendor came in or out, north wind flew to my stockinged legs, wrapping them in cold that hovered and lingered like tulle fog. "My first check, I'm getting boots," I thought, cringing as one gusty breeze followed another into the new, busy office. This was a year before females wore pants to work. I knew I would be fired if I came to work in slacks. The boots would help. Jeannie was friendly and began talking to me whenever I walked by. Even so, it came as a surprise when she invited me to dinner.

"We live right up the road from here in a little old house. Is five o'clock OK?"

"Sounds great," I smiled.

"I hope you like pasta," Jeannie said.

"I sure do." But my stomach felt like icy fingers grabbed it. What will Jeannie think of me?

"Good. I'll tell Joe you're coming. And you'll meet my baby... Gus. That's my sweet doggie. He's getting old, but he's a member of the family."

My secret was close to my lips, but the constriction in my throat stopped me. Instead, I smiled, "I'll see you tomorrow night."

"Come in. Did you find us OK?"

"Joe, this is my friend, Ruth, from work, I told you about."

"Hello," I said to Jeannie's husband, who looked quite a bit older than she.

"And this is my precious Gus," Jeannie patted a mongrel of about a hundred pounds. "He's old and he's smelly, but we love him."

"Your cooking smells wonderful," I warmed to the down-to-earth people.

The house was the smallest I'd ever been in. It reminded me of the visit I'd made to the world's fair as a child, looking through a window, standing on tiptoe and seeing eye to eye, what were then called dwarfs, in their home.

I was looking at Jeannie's sweet face and heavy body, Joe's thin frame, and felt caught, a prisoner of my thoughts.

Jeannie said, "Come on outside. I'll show you our garden. We don't have much space in back, but we've got everything you can imagine growing."

I followed docilely for the few feet it took us to walk to the yard.

"Ruth, I have a daughter. She's sixteen already! She's with her father."

"Oh!"

"Yeah, Joe's my second husband. I wanted you to know. You see this. This is what's in the sauce we're cooking. Do you know what pesto is?

"I have two daughters," I said it. The place where icicles used to lay felt lighter now, and calmly quiet.

"How nice. Where are your kids?"

"With their father," I said.

"God, you know I'm not the only one," I prayed. "Jeannie's a good person, and her daughter isn't with her."

"Taste it," Jeannie handed me something green. "This is basil."

"Mmmmmmm."

"Wait till you taste it in the sauce." We stood in the tiny yard crammed with staked plants high as the house. "Come in. I'll show you the pesto I made. I freeze it. Joe's a really good cook. Let's go see how he's doing."

Jeannie said, "Gus loves wine so be careful he doesn't drink yours," as she poured chianti into my wine glass.

"You're kidding," I laughed. Gus came smoothly by and started lapping from my glass.

"I don't believe it," I kept laughing. Gus kept lapping.

"Put your hand over your glass."

"Gus, you know you're not supposed to drink out of other people's glasses," Jeannie scolded lovingly.

I waited. No one offered me another glass. I drank and covered my glass. Joe brought the bottle and I moved my hand so he could pour.

"What does he get like when he drinks?"

"Oh, he gets happy. Then he gets sleepy. Just like us," laughed Jeannie.

The food was the best of its kind.

Satisfied, Gus walked away from the wine glasses and took a nap.

Joe hadn't said much all evening. Over Gus's snoring he said, "Ruth, do you like Western music?"

"I'm not too familiar with it."

He bent down and picked up an old album. "This here's Johnny Cash. Do you want to listen to him?"

"Sure."

He put the record on, and his toughened features softened as Cash sang.

Joe handed me the album cover. "See where this was made." I looked at the cover.

"Should I tell her?"

Jeannie's face changed from its usual softness to a harsh, lined scowl, "NO."

"She's all right. I want to tell her."

Jeannie silently resigned herself. Gus sighed and snored more loudly.

"Johnny Cash came and sang for us when I was at "Q." *

---

*San Quentin Prison

PASSION FLOWER

*Passion flower
near the flowing
waterfall
fold your petals
around me.
We are one
and all.
Passion Flower
simply be
to the music
of your being
as I am
to mine.*

L.A. Dreams

A hundred years or so after gold was discovered in California we did our journey in a station wagon to the Hollywood hills from New Jersey. With all our wedding gifts and clothing piled high in back of the car, Bob could still see the icy roads. It was the beginning of a new year and a new life.

Could it have been only seven years since seventh grade when I had written to the stars: Lana Turner, HOLLYWOOD, CA; Betty Grable, HOLLYWOOD, CA and never believing I'd hear from her: VERONICA LAKE, HOLLYWOOD, CA. The magic of it when I finally received an autographed photograph from each one! I was rich with their pictures glued carefully into my scrapbook. I knew them better than my cousins who lived in Philadelphia and Brooklyn, since three times each week mom and I walked across town to the only theatre in town—the Ritz. For ten cents admission I formed my ideas of life and love with the help of MGM and Carmen Miranda, Laurence Olivier, Vivien Leigh, Clark Gable, and the films *Lost Horizon* and something about *Pago Pago*.

The mountain pass we took that winter night on our way to Los Angeles was slippery and narrow. There was room enough for two cars to pass each other going opposite ways. Our headlights reached beyond the blackness that surrounded. The only sound was our 1949 Plymouth engine. I felt my heart beating nervously before Bob said, "I'll have to go around that truck." He sounded calmer and more determined than I'd ever heard him.

My heart again. Only now it was skipping like a jump-roper.
"But it's in the way."
"We can't stay here. I have to drive around it."
"Why does it look that way?"
"It jack-knifed on the ice."

"Oh, God."

"Don't worry. I'm an excellent driver. I'll only go five miles an hour. We have to go around it. We can't stay here."

I eyed the road. It looked smaller than the width of our wagon.

Bob responded to my thought. "Don't worry. There's enough room. We'll make it. You know that, don't you?"

I didn't know it. That's why I was so terrified. I'd never voted. I was too young. I wanted a chance to be his wife, to have our children, to live in the sun in California.

"Trust me."

Silence.

"Can you trust me?"

"Yes," I said. The word came out without any conscious help from me, just like my pulse raced and a rush of wetness spurted from my armpits like from two attached fountains.

"Yes, I trust you," I said and looked at the man I expected to live the rest of my life with. For a moment I thought of closing my eyes as Bob started to go around the forty-foot trailer-truck. No, I want to go through this with my eyes wide open.

I didn't know how to drive a car. Bob had learned to drive, when he was a young boy, sitting on his father's lap. He taught him well. That was my first realization of what a good learner Bob was.

Our two daughters are the first native Californians in the family. They were born in Los Angeles.

One hot August night, lying on the front lawn to get some cool air, all of us together, on Falling Leaf Avenue, I looked up at the heavens and thanked my lucky stars.

Music

lifts
lilts
lets soul
stray
from its
bodily attachment
and soar.

Jazzman

We were tired, more tired than we'd acknowledge to ourselves. But my friend had one more place to stop at the mall. It was called Sticks and Wicks. I liked the name and played with the images it brought to my mind.

The scents of many aromas met us as we stepped into the store. The woman near the counter said, "Someone was giving kittens away today in the mall." We looked at the floor where a cardboard box contained a champagne colored kitten with sable ears. He looked like he'd lived all of his six weeks in that cozy box with its little round white container of milk amidst a store of candles of all shapes, sizes and scents.

The lady set her pretty kitten on the carpeted floor. "I hope he will be happy. He's so young to be away from his mother." He moved around our feet and looked content.

"I've heard that keeping a ticking clock near kittens, or a hot water bag—so they feel like they're near their mother—helps them sleep."

"That's a good idea," she said. "I think I'll put a hot water bottle near him."

"Make sure he can't put his claws in it," I said.

"I hope he will be happy."

"Is he your only cat?"

"Oh, no. I have five cats at home!"

I laughed, "Then I'm sure he will be happy. They'll all be his mother to him. What are you naming him?" I asked.

She said, "Jazzman."

"That's a great name. My husband's been listening to jazz since he was about fifteen. I'll have to tell him."

She looked at me with an expression that spoke louder than words. I tried to rewind my mind to tell where we disconnected.

"Oh..." I realized, in the store permeated with essences of peach, apricot, strawberry and...yes, <u>jasmine</u>.

Rumi and I

We few poets meet
making a community at one
both the hour and the essence.

Julie, hearing the reading
of my poem "Acceptance,"
then Izabel's of Rumi,
honors me, saying I should be in Rumi's book.

And, with a little trick
of stirring up our literary juices
I find Rumi soon will be in mine.

We quote, we take words
at random to build castles of poems.

This time, by opening his book,
Rumi's thoughts leap out
from 13th century to join us
in our avid camaraderie with these words,
"Come horseback through
the spider webs of twilight."

We dare not read the rest
lest we run short on foot
and miss the spinning motion
of such a man as Rumi.
Our safety lies in sharing first
and then opening to his page again
to slip into
the eloquence of his twilight.

WHEN I REALIZED
THAT I HAD BECOME A GROWN-UP

I can date the moment of that life-changing epiphany. I see a path of many times when I grew in that direction. I've been the tortoise, not the hare. And that is just as good.

During a time I felt I should be grown-up by now (maybe you know what that's like!), I felt anything but. To my surprise, people sought me out and shared their fears, their hopes—their very souls, when I could have used some mentoring myself, and didn't know enough to seek it.

I was grateful that I could help another being. I wasn't yet grown-up. When a friend asked me if I'd ever considered getting counseling, I went for it like sponge to water.

A magnitude 7.8 earthquake hit our area. I was at the stove, cooking dinner, angry, as seasonings above pots and pans I was using were falling from their shelf above, into my cooking. My anger just as quickly turned to fear. I remembered that standing in a doorway was supposed to be safer during an earthquake. I shut the stove, took the few steps to the kitchen doorway, and felt fear well up throughout my body. I was alone and terrified.

A few moments later I heard my neighbor screaming loudly through the doorway I'd left open because it was such a hot day.

I left my protective doorway and went to her. She was smoking a cigarette, yelling and screaming, "I'm too young to die. I'm going to drive to the Bay Bridge."

I said, "If you put out your cigarette I'll hug you."

We stood on the small stone platform between our apartments, hugging our terror together, two heartbeats as one. I told her to come sit inside with me so we could talk. Aware that neither of us was in a protective doorway now, I decided that getting her calm and away from the bridge, which had collapsed, took precedent. After she calmed some, I got her to promise she wouldn't drive. Did I finally realize I had become a grown-up? I was beginning to think there was still hope.

The final thing, as nothing before, had me accept that recognition of grown-up-ness. It happened when I received a phone call from a physician in NJ telling me that my daughter had had a massive paralyzing stroke, with major brain damage.
I took the first plane available, fully a grown-up.

Il Piccolo

Not that I want to rush
off earth;
I still haven't tasted
it all.
But after my first frozen mocha
and second reading,
for a moment
I was ready or not—
a lovely place to be.

A Gift from Alice

It would probably take reams of paper to describe Alice, and I only saw her twice. The first time was when I was first in love with Bob.

He had told me about his genius friend Jack's sister, Alice, and said she was a genius, too. Before Bob and I had met, he had dated Alice a couple of times.

By about age fifteen she was supporting herself in New York City, a ghostwriter for Walter Winchell, the famous journalist.

When Bob took me to a party at Alice's NY apartment, she—a quick study—after observing me, said, "The holes in your head fit the screws in his head."

Between all the mutual life changes of marrying, divorcing, moving between states, we lost track of Alice. She seemed like an experienced mature woman of twenty-two or so, when we met, to my immature inexperienced eighteen.

After Bob and I remarried, a small, square envelope arrived one day. It was before computers became a part of life. The letter was from an agency which helped people, who were looking for people they knew, to find them—if they wanted to be found.

It was from Alice. We were very pleased to make contact again, and responded that we would like that. Southwest Airlines had a promotion of two flights for the price of one, so we took it to Thousand Oaks, where we stayed over with Alice a night or two and caught up with the decades behind us.

She, proud and envious both, of her brilliant brother Jack, who had become a clinical psychologist, went to Italy during those years, to get a medical degree. They weren't an option for females back then in the United States, so—as usual—Alice took control of her own life as best she could. Her practice was in the field of psychotherapy, using her own designed alternative approach.

She was long since divorced and had a son who was mentally challenged, and a daughter, like her, who was a genius. It was a good visit. We were glad to get back together. We kept in touch by mail, Alice and I sending our poems and letters to each other.

The years went fast. I gave Alice my sad news of Bob's passing on. She sent me some Jewish prayers for the dead, and suggested I contact the Veteran's Administration to inquire about possible death benefits. There were no benefits and the amount for cremation and their basic services took whatever I had. One day Alice phoned and asked me, "Did you get what I sent?" I thought of the prayers she had sent me. They were in Hebrew and translated into English. I remembered her instructions to light a candle and read them aloud to myself, and to do that on the anniversary of Bob's death. The tradition was called "Yur Tzight." the annual remembrance. I was not raised with Jewish traditions, but did them as Alice requested. With them she had sent a sympathy card.

By this time I had learned that the housemate who had moved in with me was a lying drug addict. Neighbors had begun reporting her strange behaviors to me, and were worrying about me. My mortgage, again, felt like a great weight on my shoulders, as I knew I would have to ask her to leave.

Alice was affluent, and I couldn't help wishing that she had enclosed a small check with her beautiful sympathy card. "Yes, Alice," I said, "I got what you sent. Thank you."

I had heard that a very nice shoppe, across from the large Stanford Shopping Center, took jewelry on consignment. I took my wedding ring to them. They admired it and the price I could expect would pay my next month's mortgage payment. A month later I went back. The ring was still there. The same woman greeted me like she could see why I'd done it. She said, "It's such a lovely ring. You should keep it."

With work and a roommate, I had been getting by, as far as my financial plights were concerned. But in those early months, even though I wrote poems about my love and loss, I was an emotional mess. I felt fortunate because my friend, Jen, whom I had met as a neighbor, who soon became a friend, is also a psychotherapist, and is widowed herself.

One day she told me, "There are times you may think you're going crazy, but you're not. We go through many different reactions when we're grieving."

I never actually thought that I was crazy. But I knew how tortured I really was, when one day I ran into one of the special education teachers with whom I enjoyed working. She had asked with concern, "How are you doing?" I said, "I'm doing fine." And, there, in the middle of Long's Drug Store, I burst into tears.

I had bought a small, green metal box, which came with category dividers. There, in one section, I had placed anything that looked important. I used to see a card that Bob had explained was for some debt he had in connection with the house we had once made payments for. When we parted he sold the house, and ended up owing the mortgage company. Bit by bit he paid on that for years.

It was during those early months after Bob died that I received something in the mail that I must have thought had to do with that old bill, even though it had my name on it.

A few nights ago, I went to the small, green metal box, looking for my daughter's social security card for her. In the one section where I'd put just about everything, I didn't see it. I reached into another section, and—to my surprise—there was a small grey booklet. It was from Glendale Federal Bank, dated March 22, 1996, four months after Bob's death. I must have placed it there, hurriedly, thinking it had something to do with that old mortgage payback, which Bob had paid in full many years ago. Maybe at that tragic time in my life, I WAS a little crazy. My name is on it, an account number, and the words, "New Account, balance $1,400." So that's what Alice had meant when she asked me if I'd gotten what she sent. She has died since then.

It seems this record has fallen by the wayside as banks merged and shifted in the past fourteen years. No one I called could trace it.

But now I know. Alice was helping me when she knew I needed help.

I'd Rather Laugh

I stole this title from a book
of that name.
I would rather laugh.
I've shared the alternative
describing how I've lived.
I would rather laugh.
I don't need to be the
loudest, longest laugher,
just so I can remember
to see, as Shakespeare did,
"All the world's a stage,
and all the men and women
merely players,"

Lately, without
the laughing catalyst
that was my clever husband,
I find that laughing at myself
can be delightful.
Like when I sat down
on the cat
and couldn't stop
the part of me
that sits
once it was into motion,
and the cat—
he didn't scratch,
he didn't act as if
this were untypical.
I picked him up
still laughing
placed him on my lap

*where he should have been
in the first place—
and he was completely
loose and limber
like a bag of rice,
laughing at my embarrassment
no doubt
with the dignified laughter of cats.*

Dumpster Shoes

One day I watched a talk show where a couple appeared nicely dressed for the occasion and had a book to promote. Their clothing had to do with the book. This wasn't a fashion show. It wasn't even one of those outlet interviews where people can learn of places to shop for less.

This couple took recycling a step deeper. They paid no monetary price. Yet they showed a table full of their valuables on TV. They had literally dived in dumpsters for them. They chose neighborhoods that would reap the finest. Their finds of things for body and home showed quality and good taste. Besides the thousands of dollars they saved, they talked of the fun they had.

"Many things we come up with," they said, "have never been used. The labels are still attached. People throw perfectly good things away," they laughed, "gifts they didn't want, lots of useful things." The couple was careful. They wore gloves and watched what they touched, they said.

I was in conversation with a woman whom I recently met. My dilemma came up about computers and whether I want to get another since the first one I had gave out. She's a poised and dignified looking person. Her son has a similar aura about his thirteen year old body.

"We found two computers, perfectly good, in a dumpster," she said.

I told her about the program I'd seen on the subject.

"We only go when we have a feeling," she said.

"I really should get a computer," I said.

"How much do you want to pay?" she asked.

Outside of our apartment, a few feet away, is a garbage shoot in an area the size of our kitchen. When I leave the apartment my hands are invariably full. My cautious husband reminds his practical wife to keep keys in purse or pocket, not in hand, when dumping a bag on the way out. I don't expect to throw my keys, which are in one hand, when I throw the bag which is in the other. But when he asks me so nicely, what can I do?

It was the day before our daughter Riki's return flight to the East Coast. We were catching up with loose ends. I wanted to take her to lunch. We needed to do laundry and I wanted to get her to the shoemaker right away. She had a pronounced awkward stretch of her left leg when she walked, as though she were searching for the correct placement of her foot. In prior visits we thought this was because of the way she was left after an accident.

I began asking mentally why that was so after she'd had chiropractic and traditional medical care. The answer came to me. When we measured her legs the answer was visible. Her left leg was half an inch shorter. No wonder!

On our way to transfer laundry to the dryer, before going to lunch and the shoemaker, we grabbed up boxes and wrapping left from the holidays. The trash dumpster is at the other end of the building. Riki held the lid so I could throw in my huge armful. I couldn't see over the biggest box as I dumped all that and reminded her to hold the cover till I got my arms away. She emptied her hands and groaned, "I threw my shoes in."

"You threw your shoes in the dumpster?"

"Yes. Soon as I did it I wondered why I was holding two bags."

"I'm not going to climb in there," I said, wondering how to get the shoes. There was no question in either of our minds of her diving in. She's shorter, heavier and a Libra, the scales of balance; I'm the Capricorn mountain goat.

We began to laugh at our ridiculous predicament.

"I'm going upstairs to get a broom. Maybe I can pick up the bag by the handles."

We looked at each other and had delicious, silly laughter again.

As I went to the third floor—no elevators there—I thought of getting the step stool, too. When I got inside I began laughing again.

Back at the dumpster I stood on my sturdy oak step stool and looked down into the nearly empty space. I reached for the bag handle with the holding end of the broom. To my very pleasant surprise, it was so easy to fish it out.

The shoemaker was able to take care of us right away. "Good, we'll come back after lunch to get them and wait while you do the pair she's wearing now." We left the dumpster shoes with him.

When my husband came home he asked if the shoemaker was able to fix both pair.

"Just one pair," I said. "The others were too far gone."

"So, did you leave them there for him to dump?"

Reflection

*I need to look back now,
before I look ahead, to the beyond,
at what I've made
of this thing called life
of what I've learned
of what I've given
of all its meaning.
I look back.*

ETERNITY

*I'd put knowing aside
like a cherished gift,
distracted by the ordinary.
It stayed as would
a vivid dream
ready to be acknowledged.
Finally in awareness
I fully felt
the gift of love
that knows
no earthly boundaries.*

Biography

Ruth put aside a scholarship to Newark State College, in New Jersey, before making California her home.

Twenty years later, after taking all the available non-credited writing classes she could find, Ruth went back to college, selecting literature, poetry, short story writing, psychology, sociology, art history, and art.

Ruth was staff writer for *Kaleidoscope*, the publication of the Peninsula Poets Guild in Northern California, and poetry judge for *The Write Place*.

She taught creative writing, and established a poetry group for psychiatric patients at Marin General Hospital, merging with the art director's class. Amazing changes came about as patients, some who had never written before, expressed their deepest feelings and discovered their own hidden joy.

Ruth's first two books of poetry are titled, *Days of Together* and *Maybe Shirts Are Easier: A Path Back to Life*.

www.ingramcontent.com/pod-product-compliance
Lightning Source LLC
Chambersburg PA
CBHW032123090426
42743CB00007B/440